MAKING
MOVIES

Sidney Lumet

Alfred A. Knopf   New York   1995

THIS IS A BORZOI BOOK
PUBLISHED BY ALFRED A. KNOPF, INC.

Library of Congress Cataloging-in-Publication Data
Lumet, Sidney.
Making movies / by Sidney Lumet. — 1st ed.
p.   cm.
ISBN 0-679-43709-6
1. Motion pictures—Production and direction—Handbooks,
manuals, etc.   I. Title.
PN1995.9.P7L86   1995
791.43′0233′092—dc20   94-34449
CIP

Manufactured in the United States of America

FIRST EDITION

For Piel

CONTENTS

PREFACE

I once asked Akira Kurosawa why he had chosen to frame a shot in *Ran* in a particular way. His answer was that if he'd panned the camera one inch to the left, the Sony factory would be sitting there exposed, and if he'd panned an inch to the right, we would see the airport—neither of which belonged in a period movie. Only the person who's made the movie knows what goes into the decisions that result in any piece of work. They can be anything from budget requirements to divine inspiration.

This is a book about the work involved in making movies. Because Kurosawa's answer stated the simple truth, most of the movies I'll discuss in this book are pictures I directed. With those, at least, I know exactly what went into each creative decision.

There's no right or wrong way to direct a movie. What I'm writing about is how *I* work. For students, take it all; take what you want and throw the rest away; or throw it all away. For a few readers, perhaps it might make up for the times a movie crew has tied you up in traffic, or shot in your neighborhood all night long. We really *do* know what we're doing: It only looks as if we don't. Serious work is going on even when it seems as if we're just standing around. For everyone else, I'll try to tell you as best I can how movies are made. It's a complex technical and emotional process. It's art. It's commerce. It's heartbreaking and it's fun. It's a great way to live.

A warning about what you *won't* find in the book: There are no personal revelations other than feelings arising from the work itself—no gossip about Sean Connery or Marlon Brando. Mostly I love the people I've worked with in what's necessarily an intimate process. So I respect their foibles and idiosyncrasies, as I'm sure they respect mine.

Finally, I must ask for an indulgence from the reader. When I began making movies, the only crew jobs available to women were as script girls and in the editing department. As a result, I still think of movie crews as male. And in fact, they still predominantly are. I've therefore developed the lifetime habit of using male pronouns. The word "actress" or "authoress" always struck me as condescending. A doctor's a doctor, right? So I've always referred to "actors" and "writers," regardless of their sex. So many movies that I've made involved police before women played any significant role on the force, so even my casts have been heavily dominated by men. After all, my first movie was called *12 Angry Men.* In those days, women could be excused from jury duty simply because they were women. The male pronouns I use almost always refer to both men and women. Most people working in the movies today have been brought up in a far more equally balanced world than I was. Hopefully, such indulgences won't have to be asked for again.

MAKING
MOVIES

THE DIRECTOR
The Best Job in the World

The entrance to the Ukrainian National Home is on Second
Avenue between Eighth and Ninth streets in New York City.
There's a restaurant on the ground floor. The odor of pierogi,
borscht, barley soup, and onions hits me as soon as I walk in.
The smell is cloying but pleasant, even welcoming, especially
in the winter. The rest rooms are downstairs, always reeking of
disinfectant, urine, and beer. I go up a flight of stairs and walk
into an enormous room the size of a small basketball court. It
has colored lights, the inevitable revolving mirrored ball, and a
bar along one wall, behind which are stacked sound amplifiers
in their suitcases, empty cartons, boxes of plastic garbage bags.
Setups are also sold here. Stacks of folding chairs and tables are
piled along the walls.

This is the ballroom of the Ukrainian National Home,
where loud, stomping accordion-accompanied dances are held
on Friday and Saturday nights. Before the breakup of the

USSR, there would be at least two "Free the Ukraine" meetings held here every week. The room is rented out as often as possible. And we have now rented it for two weeks to rehearse a movie. I've rehearsed eight or nine movies here. I don't know why I feel like this, but rehearsal halls should always be a little grungy.

Two production assistants are nervously awaiting me. They've started the coffee machine. In a plastic box, amid ice cubes, are containers of juice (freshly squeezed), milk, and yogurt. On a tray, bagels, Danish, coffee cake, slabs of wonderful rye bread from the restaurant downstairs. Butter (whipped and packaged) and cream cheese (whipped and packaged) are waiting, plastic knives alongside. Another tray holds packets of sugar, Equal, Sweet 'n Low, honey, tea bags, herb teas (every kind imaginable), lemon, Redoxon (in case anyone has the first signs of a cold). So far so good.

Of course, the PAs have set up the two rehearsal tables the wrong way. They've placed them end to end, so the twelve or so people due here in half an hour will have to sit stretched out as if in a subway car. I have them move the tables side by side, putting everybody as close together as possible. Newly sharpened pencils are lined up in front of each chair. And a fresh script. Even though the actors have had their scripts for weeks, it's amazing how often they forget them on the first day.

I like to have as much of the production team as possible at the first reading. Already present are the production designer, costume designer, second assistant director, the Directors Guild of America (DGA) trainee (an apprentice), the script girl, the editor, and the cameraman, if he's not out doing tests on locations. As soon as the tables are in place, they descend on me—all of them. Floor plans are rolled out. Swatches. Polaroids of a red '86 Thunderbird and a black '86 Thunderbird. Which do I want? We still don't have permission for the bar on Tenth Street and Avenue A. The guy wants too much money. Is there another location that will work as well? No. What should I do? Pay him the money. Truffaut has a moment in *Day for Night* that touches the heart of every director. He's just finished an arduous day's shooting. He's walking off the set. The production team surrounds him, peppering him with questions for tomorrow's work. He stops, looks to the heavens, and shouts, "Questions! Questions! So many questions that I don't have time to think!"

Slowly, the actors come wandering in. A false joviality hides their nervousness. Did you hear the one about— Sidney, I'm so glad we're working together again . . . hugs, kisses. I'm a big kisser myself, a toucher and a hugger as opposed to a groper. The producer arrives. Usually, he's the groper. His object this morning is to ingratiate himself, particularly with the stars.

Now, a huge burst of laughter rises from downstairs. One of the stars has arrived. The star is also ingratiating himself, showing what a regular guy he is. Sometimes there will be an entourage. First, a secretary. This is discouraging, because it means that on a ten-minute break, the secretary will bring in eight messages so urgent that the star will be on the phone instead of resting or studying the script. Second, the star's makeup person. Most stars have a contractual right to their own makeup person. Third, a bodyguard (whether needed or not). Fourth, a friend, who'll leave quickly. And last, there is the teamster driver. He gets a union minimum of about nine hundred a week plus overtime. And there is lots of overtime, because most stars have the earliest call in the morning and are the last to leave at night. The teamster will have nothing to do from the time he drops the star off at rehearsals until he picks the star up at night to take him home. So the first thing the teamster does is head for the coffee machine. He tries a piece of the coffee cake, then a Danish. A glass of orange juice to wash down the coffee, and then a bagel, heavily buttered to get rid of the taste of the Danish. A little egg salad, a little fruit, and finally he tiptoes back downstairs again, to do whatever it is that teamsters do all day.

Not all stars keep an entourage. Sean Connery will bound up the steps two at a time, rapidly shake hands all around, then plop himself down at the table, open his script, and start studying. Paul Newman treads slowly upstairs, the weight of the world on his shoulders, puts drops in his eyes, and makes a bad joke. Then he opens his script and starts studying. I don't know how he manages *without* a secretary. Paul leads one of the most generous and honorable lives of anyone I've ever known. Between his popcorn and salad dressing and his other merchandising, all for charities he's created, which serve people overlooked by other charities, not to mention his movie work, his days are packed. But he does it all and never seems pressed.

The unit publicity person is there too. They're annoying, publicists, but their lives are hell. The actors hate them because they're always asking for an interview on the day the actor has to shoot his most difficult scene; the studio is always letting them know that what they're sending to the West Coast is crap and unusable; the star's personal publicity people, jealously guarding their turf, want all requests to go through them; and we all know that nothing the publicists do now matters, because the picture won't be out for at least nine months and whatever photo was in the *Daily News* will have been long forgotten—and besides, the title of the movie will have been changed.

Often the last to arrive is the writer. He is last because he knows that at this point he is the target. At this moment, anything wrong can only be his fault, since nothing else has happened yet. So he moves quietly to the coffee table, stuffs his mouth full of Danish so he won't have to answer any questions, and tries to become as small as possible.

The assistant director is trying to set up the last of the medical exams for the insurance company (leading cast members are always insured). And I'm making believe I'm listening to everybody, a phony warm smile on my face, just waiting for the minute hand to reach straight up (the start of the hour) so we can begin the reason for all this: We're here to make a movie.

Finally, I can't wait any longer. It's still three minutes of, but I glance over to the AD. Nervous, but with a voice filled with authority, he says, "Ladies and gentlemen"—or "Folks" or "Hey, gang"—"can we take our seats?" The tone the AD uses is important. If he sounds like Santa Claus chortling "Ho-ho-ho," the actors know that he's afraid of them, and he'll have a rough time later. If he sounds pompous and officious, they'll surely screw him somewhere along the line. The best are the British ADs. Out of years of English good manners, they go quietly from one actor to the other: "Mr. Finney, we're ready for you now." "Miss Bergman, if you please."

The actors gather around the table. I give my first direction to them. I tell them where to sit.

Actually, I've been directing this picture for some time. Depending on how complicated the physical production of the movie will be, I've been in preproduction anywhere from two and a half to six months. And, depending on how much work had to be done on the script, perhaps for months before preproduction began. Major decisions have already been made. There are no minor decisions in moviemaking. Each decision will either contribute to a good piece of work or bring the whole movie crashing down around my head many months later.

The first decision, of course, was whether to do the movie. I don't know how other directors decide. I decide completely instinctively, very often on just one reading. This has produced very good movies and very bad ones. But it's the way I've always done it, and I'm too old to change now. I don't analyze a script as I read it for the first time. I just sort of let it wash over me. Sometimes it happens with a book. I read *Prince of the City* in book form and knew I desperately wanted to make a movie of it. I also make sure that I have the time to read a script straight through. A script can have a very different feeling if reading it is interrupted, even for half an hour. The final movie will be seen uninterrupted, so why should reading the script for the first time be any different?

Material comes from many sources. Sometimes the studio sends it with a firm offer and a start date. That, of course, is the best of all worlds, because the studio is prepared to finance the movie. Scripts arrive from writers, agents, stars. Sometimes it's material that I've developed, and then starts the agonizing process of submissions to studios and/or stars to see if financing will be forthcoming.

There are many reasons for accepting a movie. I'm not a believer in waiting for "great" material that will produce a "masterpiece." What's important is that the material involve me personally on some level. And the levels will vary. *Long Day's Journey Into Night* is everything one can hope for. Four characters come together and leave no area of life unexplored. However, I once did a picture called *The Appointment*. It had fine dialogue, by James Salter, but a dreadful story line that had been handed to him by an Italian producer. I presume Jim needed the money. The picture had to be shot in Rome. Until then, I had been having great difficulty in finding out how to use color. I'd been brought up on black-and-white movies, and almost all the movies I had made until then were in black and white. The two color movies I had done, *Stage Struck* and *The Group*, had left me dissatisfied. The color seemed fake. The color seemed to make the movies even more unreal. Why did black and white seem real and color false? Obviously, I was using it wrong or— much more serious—not using it at all.

I had seen a movie of Antonioni's called *Red Desert*. It had been photographed by Carlo Di Palma. Here, at last, was color being used for drama, for furthering the story, for deepening the characters. I called Di Palma in Rome, and he was available for *The Appointment*. I happily accepted the picture. I knew that Carlo would get me through my "color block." And he did. That was a perfectly sensible reason to do the movie.

I've done two movies because I needed the money. I've done three because I love to work and couldn't wait anymore. Because I'm a professional, I worked as hard on those movies as on any I've done. Two of them turned out to be good and were hits. Because the truth is that nobody knows what that magic combination is that produces a first-rate piece of work. I'm not being modest. There's a reason some directors can make first-rate movies and others never will. But all we can do is prepare the groundwork that allows for the "lucky accidents" that make a first-rate movie happen. Whether or not it *will* happen is something we never know. There are too many intangibles, as the following chapters will reveal.

For anyone who wants to direct but hasn't made a first movie yet, there is no decision to make. Whatever the movie, whatever the auspices, whatever the problems, if there's a chance to direct, take it! Period. Exclamation point! The *first* movie is its own justification, because it's the first movie.

I've been talking about why I decided to do a particular movie. Now comes the most important decision I have to make: What is this movie about? I'm not talking about plot, although in certain very good melodramas the plot is *all* they're about. And that's not bad. A good, rousing, scary story can be a hell of a lot of fun.

But what is it about emotionally? What is the theme of the movie, the spine, the arc? What does the movie mean to me? Personalizing the movie is very important. I'm going to be working flat out for the next six, nine, twelve months. The picture had better have some meaning to me. Otherwise, the physical labor (very hard indeed) will become twice as exhausting. The word "meaning" can spread over a very wide range. *The Appointment* meant that I had the chance to work with Carlo. And what I learned made a difference on all my subsequent pictures.

The question "What is this movie about?" will be asked over and over again throughout the book. For now, suffice it to say that the theme (the *what* of the movie) is going to determine the style (the *how* of the movie). The theme will decide the specifics of every selection made in all the following chapters. I work from the inside out. What the movie is about will determine how it will be cast, how it will look, how it will be edited, how it will be musically scored, how it will be mixed, how the titles will look, and, with a good studio, how it will be released. What it's about will determine how it is to be made.

As I said earlier, melodrama can have its own justification, because the question of "What happens next?" is one of the delights that's carried over from childhood. It was a thrilling feeling the first time we listened to "Little Red Riding Hood," and we're still thrilled when we see *The Silence of the Lambs*. That is not to say that *The Silence of the Lambs* is only about its story. Due to Ted Tally's fine writing, Jonathan Demme's extraordinary direction, and Anthony Hopkins's magnificent performance, it is also an exploration of two fascinating characters. But first and foremost, it is a nail-biter, a brilliant story that keeps you terrified and guessing.

Melodrama is a heightened theatricality that makes the implausible plausible. By going further, it seems more real. *Murder on the Orient Express* is a first-rate whodunit that keeps you completely off balance. I remember, when I first read the script, shrieking with joy when it was finally revealed that they *all* dun it. Talk about implausible! And after a bit of thought, I realized it was about something else: nostalgia. For me, Agatha Christie's world is predominantly nostalgic. Even her titles are nostalgic. *The Murder of Roger Ackroyd* (what a name!), *Murder on the Orient Express* (what a train!), *Death on the Nile* (what a river!)— everything about her work represents a time and a place that I never knew existed, and indeed, I wonder if they ever did. In subsequent chapters I hope to illustrate how the concept of nostalgia affected every single department that worked on *Orient Express*. And in the end, a forty-year-old Agatha Christie whodunit wound up with six Oscar nominations.

But there was another reason I wanted to do the picture. I had always felt that I'd seriously hurt two movies by directing them too ponderously. They were *The Group,* by Sidney Buchman, from Mary McCarthy's book, and a little-known picture I did called *Bye Bye Braverman,* by Herb Sargent, adapted from Wallace Markfield's novel *To an Early Grave.* They simply weren't made with enough lightness of spirit.

Certainly *The Group* would have benefited from a lighter

comedic feeling in its first twenty-five minutes, so that its deeper seriousness could emerge slowly. One of the book's leading characters, Kay, suffered from taking *everything* in life too seriously. The most minor problem would, in her eyes, become a crisis; the most casual remark could change her relationship to another person. Toward the end of the movie, Kay is leaning out a window, binoculars in hand, looking for German planes during World War II. She is convinced an air attack on New York is imminent. She leans out too far and falls to her death. The moment needed the kind of comic madness which turns to tragedy that, for example, Robert Altman is so good at.

Bye Bye Braverman was practically a perfect script. And I wound up with a pancake instead of a soufflé. A cast of wonderful comic actors—Jack Warden, Zohra Lampert, Joseph Wiseman, Phyllis Newman, Alan King, Sorrell Booke, Godfrey Cambridge—was left floundering like fish on the beach by a director who takes funerals and cemeteries too seriously.

I knew that *Murder on the Orient Express* had to be positively gay in spirit. Some things we are naturally talented for, and some things we have to learn. Some things we just can't do. But I was determined to get this movie gay, if I had to kill myself and everyone else to accomplish it. You've never seen anyone work so intensely on something meant to be light in spirit. But I learned. (Again, the specifics will be dealt with in later chapters.) I don't think I would have handled *Network* as well if it hadn't been for the lessons I learned on *Orient Express.*

I could go down the list of my movies, dissecting the reasons I did them. The reasons have varied from needing the money to being involved with every particle of my being, as I was with *Q & A.* The whole process of moviemaking is magical, so magical, in fact, that it often serves as sufficient justification for one to go to work. Just making the movie is enough.

One last word, however, on why I say yes to movie A and no to movie B. Over the years, critics and others have remarked that I'm interested in the judicial system. Of course I am. Some have said my theater roots show because of the number of plays I've done as movies. Of course they do. There have been a bunch of movies involving parents and children. There have been comedies, some done badly, some better, as well as melodramas and a musical. I've also been accused of being all over the place, of lacking an overwhelming theme that applies to all my work. I don't know if that's true or not. The reason I don't know is that when I open to the first page of a script, I'm a willing captive. I have no preconceived notion that I want the body of my work to be about one particular idea. No script has to fit into an overall theme of my life. I don't have one. Sometimes I'll look back on the work over some years and say to myself, "Oh, *that's* what I was interested in then."

Whatever I am, whatever the work will amount to, has to come out of my subconscious. I can't approach it cerebrally. Obviously, this is right and correct for me. Each person must approach the problem in whatever way works best for him.

I don't know how to choose work that illuminates what my life is about. I don't *know* what my life is about and don't examine it. My life will define itself as I live it. The movies will define themselves as I make them. As long as the theme is something I care about at that moment, it's enough for me to start work. Maybe work itself is what my life is about.

Having decided, for whatever reason, to do a movie, I return to that all-encompassing, critical discussion: What is the movie about? Work can't begin until its limits are defined, and this is the first step in that process. It becomes the riverbed into which all subsequent decisions will be channeled.

The Pawnbroker: How and why we create our own prisons.

Dog Day Afternoon: Freaks are not the freaks we think they are. We are much more connected to the most outrageous behavior than we know or admit.

Prince of the City: When we try to control everything, everything winds up controlling us. Nothing is what it seems.

Daniel: Who pays for the passions and commitments of the parents? They do, but so do the children, who never chose those passions and commitments.

The Fugitive Kind: The struggle to preserve what is sensitive and vulnerable both in ourselves and in the world.

The Anderson Tapes: The machines are winning.

Fail-Safe: The machines are winning.

12 Angry Men: Listen.

Network: The machines are winning. Or, to borrow from the NRA: TV doesn't corrupt people; people corrupt people.

Serpico: A portrait of a real rebel with a cause.

The Wiz: Home, in the sense of self-knowledge, is inside you. (This was true of the brilliant Garland movie *and* of L. Frank Baum's book.)

Running on Empty: Who pays for the passions and commitments of the parents?

The Seagull: Why is everyone in love with the wrong person? (It's no accident that in the last scene the principals play cards around a table, as if everyone got a bad deal and now needs a little luck.)

Long Day's Journey Into Night: I must stop here. I don't know what the theme is, other than whatever idea is inherent in the title. Sometimes a subject comes along and, as in this case, is expressed in such great writing, is so enormous, so all-encompassing, that no single theme can define it. Trying to pin it down limits something that should have no limits. I am very lucky to have had a text of that magnitude in my career. I found that the best way to approach it was to ask, to investigate, to let the play tell me.

A certain amount of this goes on in every good piece of work, of course. With *Prince of the City*, I had no idea how I felt about the leading character, Danny Ciello, until I saw the completed picture. With *Serpico*, I was constantly ambivalent about his character. He was such a pain in the ass sometimes. Always kvetching. Al Pacino made me love *him*, not the scripted character. *The Seagull* is totally ambivalent about behavior. Everyone is in love with the wrong person. The teacher Medvedenko loves Masha who loves Konstantin who loves Nina who loves Trigorin who belongs to Arkadina who is really loved by Dr. Dorn who is loved by Paulina. But none of this prevents them each from having their own dignity and pathos, despite their seeming foolishness. The ambivalence is a source of exploring each character in greater and greater depth. Each person is like all of us.

But in *Long Day's Journey Into Night*, no one is like any of us. The characters are on a downward spiral of epic, tragic proportions. To me, *Long Day's Journey* defies definition. One of the nicest things that ever happened to me happened on that picture: the last shot. The last shot of the movie is of Katharine Hepburn, Ralph Richardson, Jason Robards, and Dean Stockwell sitting around a table. Each is lost in his or her own addictive fantasy, the men from booze, Mary Tyrone from morphine. A distant lighthouse sweeps its beam across the room every forty-five seconds. The camera pulls back slowly, and the walls of the room gradually disappear. Soon the characters are sitting in a black limbo, getting tinier and tinier as the light sweeps across them. Fade out. After he saw the movie, Jason told me that he had read a letter of Eugene O'Neill's in which he describes his image of his family "sitting in blackness, around the table-top of the world." I hadn't read that letter. My heart leapt with happiness. That's what happens when you let the material tell you what it's about. But the material had better be great.

You and I may disagree about the meaning of a particular piece. That's not important. Whoever is making the movie has the right to his or her own interpretation. I've loved and admired any number of movies that I felt were about something other than what I was looking at. In *A Place in the Sun,* George Stevens made a wonderful, highly romantic love story. But the resonance of the Dreiser book on which it was based became the heart of the picture for me, though I hadn't read it at the time. It was really "An American Tragedy": the dreadful price that a man pays for his belief in the American myth. The important thing is that the interpretation by the director be committed enough so that his intention, his point of view, is clear. Each person is then free to agree, reject, or be awakened to his or her own feelings about the piece. We're not out for consensus here. We're out for communication. And sometimes we even get consensus. And that's thrilling.

Rightly or wrongly, I've chosen a theme for the movie. How do I pick the people who can help me translate it to the screen? We'll get into the specifics later, as each aspect of moviemaking is analyzed. But there is a general approach as well. For example, in the late fifties, walking down the Champs Élysées, I saw in neon a sign over a theater: *Douze Hommes en Colère—un Film de Sidney Lumet. 12 Angry Men* was now in its second year. Fortunately for my psyche and my career, I've never believed it was *un Film de Sidney Lumet.* Don't get me wrong. This isn't false modesty. I'm the guy who says "Print," and that's what determines what goes up on that screen. For those that have not been on a set: once a scene has been rehearsed on set, we begin to shoot it. Each time we shoot, it's called a take. We may shoot one take or thirty of the same moment. Whenever a take seems satisfactory in whole or in part, we call out, "Print." That means that the take will go to the lab to be developed and printed for us to look at the next day. The printed takes are what constitute the final film.

But how much in charge am I? *Is* the movie *un Film de Sidney Lumet?* I'm dependent on weather, budget, what the leading lady had for breakfast, who the leading man is in love with. I'm dependent on the talents and idiosyncrasies, the moods and egos, the politics and personalities, of more than a hundred different people. And that's just in the making of the movie. At this point I won't even begin to discuss the studio, financing, distribution, marketing, and so on.

So how independent am I? Like all bosses—and on set, I'm the boss—I'm the boss only up to a point. And to me that's what's so exciting. I'm in charge of a community that I need desperately and that needs me just as badly. That's where the joy lies, in the shared experience. Anyone in that community can help me or hurt me. For this reason, it's vital to have the best creative people in each department. People who can challenge you to work at your best, not in hostility but in a search for the truth. Sure, I can pull rank if a disagreement becomes unresolvable, but that's only as a last resort. It's also a great relief. But the joy is in the give-and-take. The joy is in talking to Tony Walton, the production designer on *Prince of the City,* about the theme of the movie and then seeing him come up with his expression of that theme. Hiring sycophants and servants is selling the picture and myself short. Yes, Al Pacino challenges you. But only to make you more honest, to make you probe deeper. You're a better director for having worked with him. Henry Fonda didn't know how to fake anything, so he became a barometer of truth against which to measure yourself and others. Boris Kaufman, the great black-and-white cinematographer, with whom I did eight movies, would writhe in agony and argue if he felt a camera movement was arbitrary and unmotivated.

God knows, I'm not arguing for a contentious set. There are directors who think they have to provoke people to get the best work out of them. I think this is madness. Tension never helps anything. Any athlete will tell you that tension is a sure way of hurting yourself. I feel the same way about emotions. I try to create a very loose set, filled with jokes and concentration. It sounds surprising, but the two things go together nicely. It's obvious that good talents have wills of their own, and these must be respected and encouraged. Part of my job is to get everybody functioning at his best. And if I've hired the best, think how much better *their* best is than that of the not-so-best.

The heart of *my* job—*the* decisive moment—comes when I say "Print," for it is then that everything we've been working for is permanently recorded. How do I know when to say it? I'm not really sure. Sometimes I'll feel tentative about a take, but I'll print it anyway. I don't have to use it. Sometimes I feel so sure that I'll print only that one take and move on to the next setup. (The setup is the preparation for the next take. Moving on to the next setup is a tremendous commitment. We have to tear down everything from the last setup, which may have taken hours of work, perhaps a day or even days, to prepare. If it's the last setup on a particular location, the decision is even more final, since we will be moving on and may not be allowed to return.) So saying "Print" is my biggest responsibility.

There have been times when I have printed the first take and moved on. This is dangerous, because accidents happen. The laboratory can ruin the film. Once, a work stoppage occurred at a lab in New York. The bastards just left the film in the tank. A whole day's work of not just my movie, but all the movies shot in New York that day was ruined. Once, the film was being delivered to the lab in a station wagon, which got into an accident. Cans of exposed negative rolled all over the street, and some cans had the tape ripped from them and those takes were ruined. Another time, on *The Anderson Tapes,* we had set up what was clearly a funeral for a mobster outside the original St. Patrick's Cathedral at Mulberry and Houston streets in Little Italy. I could sense tension developing. A number of goombahs were suddenly getting sensitive about the way their relatives were being portrayed. (I don't have to tell you that it was a shakedown.) Alan King was playing a gangster in the movie. He plunged right into the middle of a particularly hefty group of six guys. Their voices grew louder. Finally, I heard one of them: "Why do we gotta be a buncha hoods alla time! We got artists too!"

Alan: "Who?"

Goombah: "Michelangelo!"

Alan: "They already did that movie."

Goombah: "Yeah? Wit' who?"

Alan: "Chuckles Heston. It fell on its ass."

But the situation was serious. The assistant director came to tell me that he'd heard one of the local gentry muttering about "gettin' the fuckin' negative!" Our mob guys are very sophisticated in New York. So after each shot, we broke off the negative and gave it to a terrified production assistant, who quietly slipped away and brought the negative up to the Technicolor labs on the subway.

But what leads me to say "Print" is completely instinctive. Sometimes I say it because I feel inside me that it was a perfect take, which we'll never improve on. Sometimes because it's getting worse with each take. Sometimes there's no choice. You've run out of light, and you're due to shoot in Paris tomorrow. Tough luck. Print it and hope that nobody sees the compromise.

The greatest pressure in moviemaking is when you know that you've got only one take to get the shot. This happened on *Murder on the Orient Express*. Picture the following: We are in this enormous shed in a railway yard just outside Paris. Inside the shed stands a panting, snorting six-car train. A whole train! All mine! Not a toy train! A real train! It has been assembled from Brussels, where the Wagon-Lits Company keeps its old cars, and from Pontarlier in the French Alps, where French National Railways keeps its old engines. We have built a set of the Istanbul railroad station in London, transported it to Paris, and erected it in the shed, so that the shed has become the Istanbul terminal of the Orient Express. Three hundred extras are assembled on the "train platform" and in the "waiting room." The shot is as follows: The camera is on the Nike, a sixteen-foot motor-driven camera dolly. It is in its low position. As the train starts toward us, the camera "dollies" forward to meet it and is at the same time being raised to about the middle of the train's height, about six feet. The train picks up speed coming toward us as we pick up speed coming toward the train. By the time the center of the fourth car has reached us, we have a full close-up of the Wagon-Lit symbol. It's very beautiful, gold on a blue background. It fills the screen. As it passes us, we pan the camera to follow the Wagon-Lit symbol until we've turned one hundred eighty degrees and are facing in the opposite direction. We have now risen to the full height of the crane, sixteen feet, and we are shooting the train going away from us, getting smaller as it goes. Finally, we see only the two red lights of the last car as the train disappears into the blackness of the night.

Geoffrey Unsworth, the brilliant British cinematographer, had taken six hours to light this enormous area. Four of our stars—Ingrid Bergman, Vanessa Redgrave, Albert Finney, and John Gielgud—were appearing in plays in London. They finished their Saturday night performances, were flown over to Paris Sunday morning, and had to be back in London for their shows on Monday. The shot had to be done at night, since there's not much mystery and not nearly so much glamour in a train leaving a station in daylight. Besides, we had to vacate the shed for the French National Railways at 8:00 a.m. Monday. We couldn't rehearse the shot even once, because Geoff needed the train in place on the platform to light the whole scene. The end of the shed through which the train exited would be open to the exterior of the railway yards, with all modern Paris behind it, which was another reason we could have no daylight.

Peter McDonald is the finest camera operator I have ever worked with. The camera operator actually turns the wheels that point the camera in any direction. There is also a focus puller; his job, obviously, is to keep focus. But that's not so easy when the camera is moving one way, the train is moving the other, and you're going to pan the camera around on letters ("Wagon-Lit"), where it is very easy to see if the focus is not perfect. He's working at a lens stop of 2.8, which makes the focus even more difficult. In addition, there is the man driving the dolly toward an object (the train) whose speed he will never have seen, and a grip (stagehand) on the tongue (the counterweighted jib arm on which the camera, the camera operator, Geoff Unsworth, and I will be sitting). The tongue allows the camera to be raised or lowered in height. The coordination among these four men has to be perfect. Peter rehearses them over and over, but he's only guessing, because the train cannot be moving while Geoff is lighting it.

Finally, it's 4:00 a.m., and I'm getting nervous. Geoff is working his tail off, the electricians are running, everyone's trying his hardest. At 4:30, Geoff is ready. My heart skips a beat. I know now that we will have only one crack at it, because the sky will start to lighten at 5:10. There is no way we can get the train back into the shed, stop it on an exact mark, and be set to try it a second time in forty minutes. Besides, too much regular train traffic will have begun, so the necessary track switching won't be available to us. There's nothing to do but go for it. Extras in place, engine breathing, hearts pounding, we roll the camera. I call out: "Cue the train." The bilingual French assistant cues the engineer. The train starts toward us. We start toward the train. The tongue starts up, raising the camera with it. The focus puller is already starting to shift focus toward the onrushing Wagon-Lit logo on the fourth car. It's upon us so fast that it's hard to follow by eye, much less through a camera. Peter whips that camera around with a speed that makes me glad he insisted I lock my seat belt. The train bursts out of the shed and disappears into the night. Peter looks at me, smiles, gives a thumbs up. Geoff smiles, looks at me. I look down to the script girl and very quietly say: "Print."

Another element that impinges on how much in charge I am is the budget. I'm not one of those directors who says, "Screw the company; I'll spend what I have to." I'm very grateful to anyone who's given me untold millions to make a movie. I could never raise that kind of money myself. I work on the budget with the production manager and on the schedule with the assistant director. Then I do everything humanly possible to stay within those limits.

This is particularly important on pictures not funded by a major studio. Some of the pictures I've done have been combinations of private financing and the selling off of "territories." It works as follows: Let's say the picture is budgeted at $10 million. Of this, $3 million is in what we call "above-the-line" costs: property, director, producer, writer, actors. The other $7 million is for "below-the-line" costs—that is, everything else: sets, locations, trucks, studio rental, location and studio crews, catering, legal fees (which are enormous), music, editing, mixing, equipment rental, living expenses, set dressing (furniture, curtains, plants, etc.). "Below-the-line," in other words, is the cost of the physical production of the movie. You don't have major studio backing, so the producer goes to any or all of the yearly meetings in Milan, Cannes, or Los Angeles and tries to sell the distribution rights for the movie to individual distributors in France, Italy, Brazil, Japan—every country in the world. If he can hold on to the television rights, he can then sell those off country by country. Videocassette rights. Cable television rights. In this way, he slowly accumulates the $10 million needed to make the movie: $2 million from Japan, $1 million from France, $75,000 from Brazil, $15,000 from Israel. No offer is too small.

For this to work, however, two things are necessary. First, the producer must have an American distribution deal, a guarantee that the movie will be released in the United States. The second necessity is a completion bond, which is exactly what it says. Given by a company with ample financial resources, the completion bond guarantees that the picture will be completed. If the leading actor dies, if a hurricane destroys the set, if a fire burns the studio down, they, the completion bond company, having extracted what moneys they can from the insurance company, will finance the completion of the movie. But part of their contract—and this is standard—reads that if the production is falling behind schedule and/or running over budget *while shooting,* the bonding company can take over the movie! They have the right to then save money any way they like. If the original scene took place at the opera with six hundred extras, they can demand that you shoot it in the men's room of the opera house. If you refuse, they can fire you. If you were going to mix the sound track in surround stereo, they can make you do a monaural mix, because it costs much, much less. They own the movie at that point. Their fee, by the way, is anywhere from 3 to 5 percent of the budget of the movie.

I ask again, how free am I? Interestingly enough, I don't mind limitations. Sometimes they even stimulate you to better, more imaginative work. A spirit may develop among the crew and cast that adds to the passion of the movie, and this can show up on-screen. On certain pictures, I've worked for union minimum, and so have the actors. We did *Long Day's Journey Into Night* that way. We did it because we loved the material and wanted to see the picture made no matter what. We formed a cooperative, Hepburn, Richardson, Robards, Stockwell, and myself, each of us working for the same minimal salary. We divided the profits (there actually were some profits) in equal shares among ourselves. Total cost of the picture: $490,000. *The Pawnbroker* was done this way. Total cost: $930,000. *Daniel, Q & A, The Offense* were all done this way. These are among the most artistically satisfying pictures I've done. At other times, because I felt the picture had little commercial potential and have been grateful that a studio put up the money, I've done the unthinkable. I've taken less money than my "established price," as I did on *Running on Empty*. I've never regretted it.

I've found also that actors are very willing to go along with these arrangements if they love the material, feel it's risky, and know that everyone else will be going along on the same basis. In addition to the *Long Day's Journey* cast, Sean Connery has gone for a minimum level on this kind of adventure. Nick Nolte has, as have Timothy Hutton, Ed Asner, the brilliant production designer Tony Walton, the superb cinematographer Andrzej Bartkowiak. Sometimes I've even asked crew members to do it; some have, some haven't. But guess who have never gone along. The teamsters.

Many of the money-saving techniques I've learned on low-budget movies can and should be used on normally budgeted movies. Lots of economies can be made, with no sacrifice of quality. For example, I shoot a scene, whether in the studio or on location, by finishing off each wall. Envision the following: A room has four walls—let's call them wall A, wall B, wall C, wall D. Starting with my widest shot against wall A, I keep shooting every shot in which wall A is the background. I keep moving in against wall A until the last close-up against that wall has been shot. Then we shift to wall B and go through the same process. Then wall C, then wall D. The reason for this is that whenever the camera has to change its angle more than 15 degrees, it's necessary to relight. Lighting is the most time consuming (and therefore most expensive) part of moviemaking. Most relighting takes minimally two hours. Four relightings take an entire day! Just moving to shoot against wall A, then turning around 180 degrees to shoot against wall C is usually a four-hour job, a half day's work!

Of course, the actors are shooting completely out of sequence. But that's one of the benefits of rehearsal. I rehearse for a minimum of two weeks, sometimes three, depending on the complexity of the characters. We had no money to make *12 Angry Men.* The budget was $350,000. That's right: $350,000. Once a chair was lit, everything that took place in that chair was shot. Well, not quite. We went around the room three times: once for normal light, a second time for the rain clouds gathering, which changed the quality of the light coming from the outside, and the third time when the overhead lights were turned on. Lee Cobb arguing with Henry Fonda would obviously have shots of Fonda (against wall C) and shots of Cobb (against wall A). They were shot seven or eight days apart. It meant, of course, that I had to have a perfect emotional memory of the intensity reached by Lee Cobb seven days earlier. But that's where rehearsals were invaluable. After two weeks of rehearsal, I had a complete graph in my head of where I wanted each level of emotion in the movie to be. We finished in nineteen days (a day under schedule) and were $1,000 under budget.

Tom Landry said it: It's all in the preparation. I hate the Dallas Cowboys, and I'm not too crazy about him and his short-brimmed hat. But he hit the nail on the head. It *is* in the preparation. Do mountains of preparation kill spontaneity? Absolutely not. I've found that it's just the opposite. When you know what you're doing, you feel much freer to improvise.

On my second picture, *Stage Struck,* a scene between Henry Fonda and Christopher Plummer took place in Central Park. I had shot most of the scene by lunchtime. We broke for an hour, knowing that we had just a few shots to do after lunch to finish the sequence. During lunch, snow started to fall.

When we came back, the park was already covered in white. The snow was so beautiful, I wanted to redo the whole scene. Franz Planner, the cameraman, said it was impossible because we'd be out of light by four o'clock. I quickly restaged the scene, giving Plummer a new entrance so that I could see the snow-covered park; then I placed them on a bench, shot a master and two close-ups. The lens was wide open by the last take, but we got it all. Because the actors were prepared, because the crew knew what it was doing, we just swung with the weather and wound up with a better scene. Preparation allows the "lucky accident" that we're always hoping for to happen. It has happened many times since: in a scene between Sean Connery and Vanessa Redgrave in the real Istanbul for *Murder on the Orient Express;* in a scene between Paul Newman and Charlotte Rampling in *The Verdict;* and in many scenes with Al Pacino and various bank employees in *Dog Day Afternoon.* Because everyone knew what he or she was doing, practically all of the improvisation wound up in the finished movie.

So—on to specifics. Shall we talk about writers?

2

THE SCRIPT
Are Writers Necessary?

I've detailed the reasons why I said yes or no to a script. That meant, obviously, that a script existed.

Now, everyone in movies has what in trade jargon is called a "hot" period. That's when everybody wants you because your last movie was a hit. If you've had two hits in a row, you're sizzling. Three hits and it's "What do you want, baby? Just name it." Before you say, "Hollywood—what do you expect?" I think you should check your own profession. From my observations, the same pattern is true of publishing, the theater, music, law, surgery, sports, television—anything.

During some of my hot periods, and even some cooler ones, a script arriving from a studio usually has an accompanying letter that almost always includes the same phrase: "Of course we know the script needs work. And if you feel that the present writer can't do it, we're prepared to put on anyone you want." I've always been amazed at that. It's always a bad sign.

To me, it indicates that they have no conviction about what they bought in the first place.

The contempt that writers have endured from studios through the years is too well known to discuss again here. Most of the horror stories were true, as when Sam Spiegel had two writers working on the same picture on two different floors of the Plaza Athénée in Paris. Or when Herb Gardner and Paddy Chayefsky, who had adjoining offices at 850 Seventh Avenue in New York, one day received identical offers for a rewrite on the same script. The producer was too dumb or too preoccupied to notice that scripts were being sent to the same address, one to Room 625 and the other to Room 627. The writers typed identical letters, turning down the offer.

I come from the theater. There, the writer's work is sacred. Carrying out the writer's intention is the primary objective of the entire production. The word "intention" is used in the sense of expressing the writer's reason for having written the play. In fact, as defined in the Dramatists Guild contract, the writer has final say over everything—casting, sets, costumes, director—including the right to close the play *before it opens* if he is dissatisfied with what he sees onstage. I know of one instance when this happened. I was brought up with the concept that the one who had the initial idea, who suffered through the agony of getting it down on paper, was the one who had to be satisfied.

When I first meet with the scriptwriter, I never *tell* him anything, even if I feel there's a lot to be done. Instead I ask him the same questions I've asked myself: What is this story about? What did you see? What was your *intention?* Ideally, if we do this well, what do you hope the audience will feel, think, sense? In what mood do you want them to leave the theater?

We are two different people trying to combine our talents,

so it's critical that we agree on the intention of the screenplay. Under the best of circumstances, what will emerge is a *third* intention, which neither of us saw at the beginning. Under the worst of circumstances, an agonizing process of cross-purposes can occur, which will result in something aimless, muddy, or just plain bad winding up on the screen. I once knew a director who always prided himself on having a secret agenda that he thought he could "sneak into" the movie. He probably envied the writer's talent.

Arthur Miller's first and, I think, only novel, *Focus,* was, in my opinion, every bit as good as his first produced play, *All My Sons.* I once asked him why, if he was equally talented in both forms, he chose to write plays. Why would he give up the total control of the creative process that a novel provides to write instead for communal control, where a play would first go into the hands of a director and then pass into the hands of a cast, set designer, producer, and so forth? His answer was touching. He said that he loved seeing what his work evoked in others. The result could contain revelations, feelings, and ideas that he never knew existed when he wrote the play. It's what we all hope for.

Once we've agreed on the all-important question "What's this picture about?" we can start in on the details. First comes an examination of each scene—in sequence, of course. Does this scene contribute to the overall theme? How? Does it contribute to the story line? To character? Is the story line moving in an ever increasing arc of tension or drama? In the case of a comedy, is it getting funnier? Is the story being moved forward by the characters? In a good drama, the line where characters and story blend should be indiscernible. I once read a very well-written script with first-rate dialogue. But the characters had nothing specific to do with the story line. That particular story could've happened to many different kinds of people. In drama, the characters should determine the story. In melodrama, the story determines the characters. Melodrama makes story line its highest priority, and everything is subservient to story. For me, farce is the comic equivalent of melodrama and comedy the comic equivalent of drama. Now, in drama, the story must reveal and elucidate the characters. In *Prince of the City,* Danny Ciello had a fatal flaw that made the ending of the movie inevitable. As a man, as a character, he was a manipulator. He felt he could handle anything and turn it to his advantage. The movie tells the story of a man like that getting into a situation he *couldn't* handle. No one could have. It was too big, too complex, with too many unpredictable elements, including other people, for anyone to control. Inevitably, it would all come crashing down around him. He created the situation, and the situation stripped him down to his essence. Character and story were one and the same.

I think inevitability is the key. In a well-made drama, I want to feel: "Of course—that's where it was heading all along." And yet the inevitability mustn't eliminate surprise. There's not much point in spending two hours on something that became clear in the first five minutes. Inevitability doesn't mean predictability. The script must still keep you off balance, keep you surprised, entertained, involved, and yet, when the denouement is reached, still give you the sense that the story *had* to turn out that way.

From a scene-by-scene breakdown, we move on to a line-by-line examination. Is the line of dialogue necessary? Revelatory? Is it saying it in the best possible way? In case of disagreement, I usually go along with the writer's decision. After all, he *wrote* it. It's also important that as director I understand each and every line. There's nothing more embarrassing than an actor asking

the meaning of a line and the director not knowing the answer. It happened to me once, on a picture called *Garbo Talks*. I
suddenly realized that I didn't know the answer to the question the actor asked. The writer had gone back to California. I
twisted and turned, bullshitting my way into an aspect of the
character that the actor was thrilled to play. Later, looking at
an earlier draft of the screenplay, I realized that a typo had
crept in between drafts. The line meant the exact opposite of
what I had explained to the actor. Not that I owned up to it.

On *Long Day's Journey Into Night,* I used the text of the play. The
only adaptation made for the screen was to cut seven pages of
a 177-page text during rehearsals. And we cut those because I
knew I was going to shoot those sections in close-ups. The use
of close-ups would make those moments clearer sooner.

Dog Day Afternoon was a completely different experience. The
script was based on an actual incident. The producer, Marty
Bregman, Pacino, and I had accepted a very good screenplay by
Frank Pierson. Structurally perfect, with fine, biting dialogue,
it was funny, compassionate, and very, very spare. By the third
day of rehearsal, I had become nervous about an area that had
nothing to do with the quality of the script or the actors. Here
was a story that, in plot, was about a man robbing a bank so his
boyfriend could have the money for a sex-change operation.
Pretty exotic stuff for 1975. Even *The Boys in the Band* had gotten
nowhere near that aspect of gay life.

I come from a working-class background. I remember going
as a child to the Loew's Pitkin, on Pitkin Avenue in Brooklyn.
It wasn't the most sophisticated crowd that piled in on Saturday night. I remember rude remarks being yelled down from
the balcony at Leslie Howard in *The Scarlet Pimpernel.*

As I said earlier, *Dog Day Afternoon* was a movie about what we
have in common with the most outrageous behavior, with

"freaks." This was a movie in which I wanted the most emotionally moving moment to occur when Pacino is dictating his will before venturing outside the bank, where he's almost certain he'll be killed. The will contained a beautiful and actual line: "And to Ernie, who I love as no man has ever loved another man, I leave . . ." This was going to be played to the same kind of audience that filled Loew's Pitkin on Saturday night. God knows what might come down from that balcony. The goal of the whole picture was toward making that line work. But could we do it?

With Frank's agreement, on the third day of rehearsal I told the actors that we were dealing with material that was sensationalist by its nature. Normally, I'm not concerned about audience reaction. But when you touch on sex and death, two aspects of life that hit a deep core, there's no way of knowing what an audience will do. They could laugh at the wrong places, catcall, start trying to talk back to the screen—any of a hundred defenses that people throw up when they're embarrassed, when what's on the screen is getting too close, or when they're looking at something they've never confronted before. I told the actors that the only way we could preclude this was to portray the characters they played as close to themselves as possible, to take as little as possible from the outside, to spare nothing of themselves from the inside. No costumes. They would wear their own clothes. "I want to see Shelly and Carol and Al and John and Chris up there," I said. "You're just temporarily borrowing the names of the people in the script. No characterizations. Only you." One of the actors asked if they could use their own words when they wanted to. For the first time in my career, I said, "Yes."

It was a remarkable group. Pacino led them with a mad courage I've seen only two other times. Katharine Hepburn, in

Long Day's Journey Into Night, and Sean Connery, in a little-known film we did called *The Offense,* took equally wild risks in their performances. And Frank Pierson's ego was healthy enough that he could see what we were reaching for. Nor were we throwing the movie open to anarchy. I had recording equipment brought into the rehearsal hall. We improvised. Each night after rehearsal, the improvisations were typed up, and eventually the dialogue was created out of those improvisations. The wonderful scene on the telephone between Pacino and his male lover, played by Chris Sarandon, was improvised in rehearsal, sitting around a table. His following phone call to his wife was made up of Al's improvisations and Susan Peretz's (playing his wife) using the original lines from the script. It's one of the most remarkable fourteen minutes of film I've ever seen. On three occasions, I left the improvisations for the day of actual shooting: two of the scenes between Al and Charles Durning as the cop in charge; and the extraordinary scene of Pacino throwing money to the crowd and feeling his power for the first time after a lifetime of failure, the scene that wound up with him shouting "Attica—Attica." I'd estimate that 60 percent of the screenplay was improvised. But we faithfully followed Pierson's construction scene by scene. He won an Academy Award for the screenplay. And he deserved it. He was selfless and devoted to the subject matter. The actors may not have said exactly what he wrote, but they spoke with his intention.

The real bank robbery had taken place over a nine-hour time period. Needless to say, live television coverage was extensive. One of the robber's friends sold a local television station a videotape of a mock wedding between John and Ernie—the real-life characters—in Greenwich Village. I saw the tape: John wore his army uniform, Ernie a wedding dress. Behind them were twenty guys in drag. Bridesmaids. They were married by a gay priest, who had come out and was subsequently defrocked. John's mother sat in the front row. The ring John put on Ernie's finger was made from a camera flashbulb. The original script had a scene in which that tape was played on television. The hostages in the bank are watching, and they see Sonny's male lover for the first time.

Given my apprehensions about how this would play at the Loew's Pitkin, I felt that if I reenacted the tape in the movie, we were dead. We'd never recover. That balcony crowd would never allow themselves to take Pacino or the movie seriously again. They'd go out of control—perhaps howl with laughter. So I cut the scene. I didn't even shoot it. Instead I had a still picture of Ernie shown on TV, which preserved the content of the scene without taking an unacceptable risk.

In every director's contract there is a clause that says he will "substantially" shoot the approved script. Because most scripts go through many changes, the last draft submitted before filming begins is the "shooting script." If the studio has any objections, they have time to voice them before principal photography starts.

Two weeks into shooting, the production manager came up to me and said that one of the high studio execs in California wanted to talk to me. I said that I was shooting and I'd call back at the lunch break. A minute later the production manager was back at my side. "He said to stop shooting. He has to talk to you." Uh-oh.

I went into the production office and picked up the phone.

Me: "Hi. What's so urgent?"

High Studio Exec: "Sidney, you have *euchred* us!"

I'd never heard the word "euchred" before. I figured it meant "screwed."

Me: "What do you mean, euchred?"

High Studio Exec: "You've cut one of the best and most important scenes in the movie."

I realized they'd been relying on that scene to create notoriety for the picture, which was precisely why I had cut it. I pointed out that they'd had the final draft for over two weeks and I hadn't heard a word from them. There was no way I could go back to re-create the wedding on tape, because we'd already shot the scene where the tape would have been played. He hung up on me.

When the studio people saw the first cut, they were ecstatically happy. The high studio exec was completely graceful, saying he understood now why I'd cut the scene.

Except in two cases, every writer I've worked with has wanted to work with me again. I think one of the reasons is that I love dialogue. Dialogue is not uncinematic. So many of the movies of the thirties and forties that we adore are constant streams of dialogue. Of course we remember James Cagney squashing a grapefruit into Mae Clarke's face. But does that evoke more affectionate memory than "Here's lookin' at you, kid"? God knows Chaplin trying to eat corn on a mechanized feeder in *Modern Times* is a great sight gag. But I don't think I've ever laughed harder than when, at the end of *Some Like It Hot,* Joe E. Brown says to Jack Lemmon, "Well—nobody's perfect."

The point is that there's no war between the visual and the aural. Why not the best of both? I'll go further. I love long speeches. One of the reasons the studio resisted doing *Network* was that Paddy Chayefsky had written at least four four-to-six-page monologues for Howard Beale, played by Peter Finch. And to top it off, he'd given a very long speech to Ned Beatty as the head of the world's largest corporation, trying to get Howard Beale on his side. But the scenes were visually arresting and brilliantly acted. Another instance is Nick Nolte's three-page speech in *Q & A,* which sets up his whole character as well as the theme of the picture. Using *Long Day's Journey Into Night* or *Henry V* as examples might be a bit unfair, but again, the speeches were handled so well visually that they remain completely satisfying in a movie. Is there anything more moving than Henry Fonda's last speech in *The Grapes of Wrath?* For sheer lyric beauty, how about Marlon Brando's speech in *The Fugitive Kind?* And Albert Finney's summing up of the case in *Murder on the Orient Express* lasted *two reels* (about seventeen minutes).

In the early days of television, when the "kitchen sink" school of realism held sway, we always reached a point where we "explained" the character. Around two-thirds of the way through, someone articulated the psychological truth that made the character the person he was. Chayefsky and I used to cal this the "rubber-ducky" school of drama: "Someone once took his rubber ducky away from him, and that's why he's a deranged killer." That was the fashion then, and with many producers and studios it still is.

I always try to eliminate the rubber-ducky explanations. A character should be clear from his present actions. And his behavior as the picture goes on should reveal the psychological motivations. If the writer has to state the reasons, something's wrong in the way the character has been written. Dialogue is like anything else in movies. It can be a crutch, or when used well, it can enhance, deepen, and reveal.

What do I owe the writer? A thorough investigation and then a committed execution of his intentions. What does the writer owe me? The selflessness that Frank Pierson showed on *Dog Day Afternoon* or that Naomi Foner showed on *Running on Empty.*

Naomi is a fine, talented, and original writer. Somehow she fell in love with a scene that, to me, was her only bad idea in the whole movie. The young boy, played by River Phoenix, comes into a strange house, sits down at the piano, and begins to play a Beethoven sonata. Eventually he notices that he is being watched by a young girl, about his age. In the script, he segues into boogie-woogie piano music.

I explained to Naomi why I thought it was a bad idea. There was a feeling of pandering to an audience: See, he's not *really* an egghead—he likes jazz, just like you and me. I'd seen the same scene as far back as José Iturbi tickling the ivories in some remote Gloria Jean movie or Jeanette MacDonald singing swing in *San Francisco.* Naomi fought for it, so I decided to leave it in to see how it played in rehearsal. When I began to stage the scene, River asked if we could cut that bit. He felt false playing it. I saw Naomi pale. We started to talk about it. River told Naomi with great simplicity and earnestness how it compromised his character. (It was enchanting to see this seventeen-year-old arguing with a serious writer twice his age.) Finally, I suggested we try it for a few days to see if there *was* a value to it. At the end of rehearsal, Naomi came over to me. She said she didn't mind if *I* had to stretch to accommodate the scene, but she couldn't bear to see River turning himself inside out to make it work. She loved the scene, but she said, "Let's cut it."

Sometimes the relationship between actors and writers gets very testy indeed. As the director, I have to be very careful here. I need them both. Most writers hate actors. And yet stars are the keys to getting a picture approved by a studio. Some directors have enormous power, but nobody has the power of one of the top stars. If the star demands it, any studio will drop the writer in less than thirty seconds—and the director too, for that matter. Most of the time, I've done enough work ahead of time so that this sort of crisis never arises. I'll come to an agreement with the writer before an actor has been approached, and I'll usually have a thorough discussion with the star about the script before we decide to go ahead. These experiences vary. Most actors, despite Hitchcock's pronouncement, are very bright. Some are superb on script. Sean Connery, Dustin Hoffman, Jane Fonda, Paul Newman are wonderfully helpful. One can gain a lot by listening to them. Pacino isn't terrifically articulate, but he's got a built-in sense of the truth. If a scene or a line bothers him, I pay attention. He's probably right.

But stars can also destroy a script. David Mamet did the first adaptation of *The Verdict.* A *major* star became interested in doing the movie, but he felt that his character had to be fleshed out more. That sometimes means explaining what should be left unsaid, a version of the rubber ducky. The *performance* should flesh out the character. Mamet always leaves a great deal unsaid. He wants the actor to flesh it out. So he refused to do it. Another writer was brought in. The writer was very bright, and she simply filled in what had been unspoken in Mamet's script and picked up a fat fee.

The script collapsed. The star then asked if he could work on it with a third writer. They did five additional rewrites. By now there was a million dollars in script charges on the picture. The scripts kept getting worse. The star was slowly shifting the emphasis on the character. Mamet had written a drunk hustling his way from one seedy case to another until one day he sees a chance for salvation and, filled with fear, takes it.

The star kept eliminating the unpleasant side of the character, trying to make him more lovable so that the audience would "identify" with him. That's another misdirected cliché of movie writing. Chayefsky used to say, "There are two kinds of scenes: the Pet the Dog scene and the Kick the Dog scene. The studio always wants a Pet the Dog scene so everybody can tell who the hero is." Bette Davis made a great career kicking the dog, as did Bogart, as did Cagney (how about *White Heat*—is that a great performance or not?). I'm sure the audience identified with Anthony Hopkins in *The Silence of the Lambs* as much as with Jodie Foster. Otherwise there wouldn't have been the roar of laughter that greeted the wonderful line "I'm having an old friend for dinner."

When I received yet another script of *The Verdict,* I reread Mamet's version, which he'd given me months earlier. I said I would do it if we went back to that script. We did. Paul Newman read it, and we were off and running.

Sometimes it's the writer who turns out to be a complete whore. I was doing a movie that needed an articulate, crisp, cerebral delivery to make the dialogue of the leading character work. Another *very* big star had gotten hold of the script and wanted to do it. I said to the writer that though the actor was terrific, I wasn't sure he could handle this kind of dialogue. The writer blanched when I said that I was going to ask the actor to read (i.e., audition) for me. I called the actor, told him that for both our sakes I thought it best if we read the script aloud. We set a date.

As I hung up the phone, the writer—who was also the producer on the picture—approached me with a mixture of awe and menace. The menace won out. In a voice that would've made a Mafia don seem like an angel, the writer-producer said, "You know, if you turn him down, the studio just might want to get rid of *you!*" The writer-producer (we call it a hyphenate) was going to get that picture made, even at the cost of ruining what had been written.

The actor read, agreed the part was wrong for him, and left

with no hard feelings at all. In fact, we did another picture together some years later. But I never worked with the writer again.

When we did *Network*, Paddy Chayefsky knew what he wanted. After all the difficulties in getting the picture OK'd, I knew he was in no mood for any rewrites demanded by stars. I'd heard, too, that Faye Dunaway could be difficult. (This turned out to be totally untrue. She was a selfless, devoted, and wonderful actress.) As always, if there's a potential problem, I like to bring it out in the open before we begin. So I made an appointment to see her. Crossing the floor of her apartment, before I'd even reached her, I said, "I know the first thing you're going to ask me: Where's her vulnerability? Don't ask it. She has none." Faye looked shocked. "Furthermore, if you try to sneak it in, I'll get rid of it in the cutting room, so it'll be wasted effort." She paused just a second, then burst out laughing. Ten minutes later I was begging her to do the part. She said yes. She never tried to get sentimental in the part, and she took home an Academy Award. My point is that it's so important to thrash these things out in advance. If push comes to shove, you can then say the obvious truth: "This is a script we both said yes to. So let's do it."

As you can gather, I like the writer present at rehearsals. Words are critical. And most actors aren't writers, nor are most directors. The improvisations in *Dog Day Afternoon* worked because I wanted the actors using themselves, not characterizing. Normally, I use improvisation as an acting *technique*, not as a source of dialogue. If the actor is having trouble finding the emotional truth of a scene, an improvisation can be invaluable. But that's about the limit.

Most writers are so used to being slapped around that they're stunned that I want them at rehearsal. Only twice has this backfired. Once, the writer fell in love with the leading lady. He showed his love by trying to make her feel as insecure as possible. He was hoping she'd ask him to help her with her part at night. She complained to me, and I had to ask him to leave. The second case involved a writer who was ready to surrender anything he wrote so that the star of the picture might hire him the next time he needed a rewrite. If the star asked a simple question, such as "I'm not sure the time of day is clear here," the writer would go downstairs, we'd hear the clackety-clack of his portable, and he'd be back with the scene rewritten to take place in a watch factory. It got embarrassing. The actors began to refer to him as "Round Heels." At the end of a week I told him the script was frozen and that he was free to go home.

Many of my relationships with writers have been just the opposite. My respect for them would grow so great during our working time that I'd want them in on every aspect of the production. Chayefsky, who was also a producer of *Network*, was a formidable talent. Beneath that comic exterior was a really funny guy. His cynicism was partly a pose, but a healthy dose of paranoia was also in his character. He told me that *Network* got made only because it was part of a settlement of a lawsuit that he'd brought. I don't know if this was true, but he *was* litigious. His answer to conflicts very often was, "Can I sue?"

He was a man who cared passionately about his work and about Israel. When we were casting, I suggested Vanessa Redgrave. He said he didn't want her. I said, "She's the best actress in the English-speaking world!" He said, "She's a PLO supporter." I said, "Paddy, that's blacklisting!" He said, "Not when a Jew does it to a Gentile."

He clearly knew more about comedy than I did. In a scene where Howard Beale comes wandering into the building looking like a lunatic, mumbling in wet pajamas and a raincoat, the guard had a line as he opened the door: "Sure thing, Mr. Beale." In my heavy-handed way, I told the guard to take in Peter Finch's disheveled state, then humor him as he said the line. Paddy was at my ear in a second. "This is TV," he whispered. "He shouldn't even notice him." He was right, of course. The line got the laugh it deserved. It wouldn't have been funny delivered my way.

But in the marvelously written and acted scene when William Holden tells Beatrice Straight he's in love with someone else, Paddy started toward me with a comment. I held up my hand and said, "Paddy, please. I know more about divorce than you do."

We had a wonderful give-and-take during both rehearsal time and shooting time. There were no problems from the first reading of the script through the opening of the movie. Paddy came to rushes (when we look at the previous day's work), and I invited him into the cutting room. By that time he was happy as could be, and he declined. After the first rough cut of the picture, we sat together with the script and made maybe ten minutes of dialogue cuts, and that was it.

When I look around at some of the absurdities in our lives, at the grotesque times we live through, I constantly wonder what Paddy might have done with them. He would've had too much to write about. I miss him every day.

Another wonderful experience was working with Edgar Doctorow on *Daniel.* Some years ago, I was invited to Paris for a retrospective of my films at the Cinémathèque. At supper after the screening, many of the French directors were complaining about the lack of writers. I pointed out as gently as I could that they might be at fault. Because of the "auteur" nonsense, with the all-powerful director, most self-respecting writers would, of course, resist getting involved in a movie. I said that not only did we have wonderful screenwriters in America, but some of our finest novelists were interested in writing for movies. Doctorow, Bill Styron, Don DeLillo, Norman Mailer, James Salter, and John Irving have written screenplays, both adaptations of their own novels and originals. Edgar was a case in point. He'd written a screenplay of his novel *The Book of Daniel* at least seven years before we got the money to make the picture. I had read it back then and thought it was one of the best screenplays I'd ever seen. Over the years, whenever I was hired to do a picture for a studio, I submitted *Daniel* as a second picture. Finally, a terrific guy named John Heyman came along. He's one of those powerful men behind the financing of studios. He knows how to finance through a British bank, registered in the Bahamas, which then sends the money to Paramount Pictures on a boat of Panamanian registry, and somehow everybody makes money. After he went into business for himself, he sent me a script that I thought was terrific, and in turn I sent him *Daniel*. He loved it. At last we were going to make the movie.

Doctorow was thrilled, though he worried that the picture might be injured once it was turned over to a studio for distribution. I told him this couldn't happen, because contractually I had final cut: Final cut means that whatever I hand in as the final picture cannot be touched in any audio or visual component. This is the last thing any studio wants to give up, so it's very difficult to achieve. I'd had final cut for many years, since *Murder on the Orient Express*. In those years, I don't think more than ten directors had it. Before we had begun rehearsals on *Daniel,* Edgar asked me to share final cut with him. I explained that final cut was one of the most difficult things for a director to achieve, and was therefore precious. I also told him that directors' contracts were always built on precedents. If I shared the cut with him, I would face similar demands in the future, and before I knew it, what had taken twenty movies to achieve would be dissipated.

I did promise him, however, that nothing he disapproved of would wind up on the screen. This was only due him. He's one of our finest novelists, and I knew how close to his heart *The Book of Daniel* was. He had written the screenplay on spec—that is, with no assurance that it would ever get done—and now, for the first time, he had to join in a collaborative venture. He had written a play that Mike Nichols had directed, but that was conceived as a play. It wasn't an adaptation of a previous work.

Edgar accepted my explanation, and we set to work. He was present at casting, rehearsals, and as much of the shooting as he wanted to be. On the first day of shooting, I shot his amazing scene where the children are handed over the heads of the crowd at a fund-raising rally for their parents. I had six cameras and five thousand extras. I looked over to him just before we rolled the cameras. He was weeping. It had been a long wait for him.

He was present at the rushes. And I asked him to join me in the cutting room, only the second time I'd ever done that. The picture was difficult to edit because in both the book and the screenplay, Doctorow had fractured time, so that past, present, and out-of-time narrations addressed to the audience were all mixed up. Together we argued, discussed, asked, doubted, were tired, exhilarated, or depressed. We went on the road when the picture opened to do publicity for it. For me, and for Edgar, it was a first-rate collaboration. Despite its critical and financial failure, I think it's one of the best pictures I've ever done.

Generally, I don't invite the writer to the rushes or the editing room, for reasons I'll discuss in a later chapter. But if it's possible, I want the writer to see the first cut. First cuts of a picture always have to have some time taken out of them. Most writers are able to see repetitions in their own work. Because of the camera, some of what's been written may become clear sooner. And in a disciplined final cut, any duplication should go. The writer can be helpful in this process.

In a sense, a movie is constantly being rewritten. The various contributions of the director and the actors, the music, sound, camera, decor, and editing, are so powerful that the movie is always changing. All these factors add digressions, increase or subtract from clarity, change the mood, or tip the balance of the story. It's like watching a column of water whose color keeps changing as different dyes are added. I think it's important for the writer to understand and, ideally, enjoy the process. In movies it's inevitable, and as long as the primary intention has been kept, the new elements should be welcomed.

At the beginning of this chapter I mentioned that on the best of movies a third intention emerges, which neither the writer nor the director can foresee. I don't know why this happens, but it does. On every movie I've done that I felt was really good, a strange amalgam was reached that surprised both the writer and me. This is the surprise that Arthur Miller talked about. Of course, the original intent is present. But all of the individual contributions from all the different departments add up to a total far greater than their individual parts. Moviemaking works very much like an orchestra: the addition of various harmonies can change, enlarge, and clarify the nature of the theme.

In that sense, a director is "writing" when he makes a picture. But I think it's important to keep the words specific.

Writing is writing. Sometimes the writer includes directions in the script. He gives long descriptions of characters or of physical settings. Close-ups, long shots, and other camera directions may be written into the script. I read these carefully, because they are reflections of the writer's intention. I may follow them literally or find a completely different way of expressing the same intention. Writing is about structure and words. But the process I've been describing—of the sum being greater than the parts—that's shaped by the director. They're different talents.

Some people can do both, but I've never known anyone who wasn't better at one than the other. To me, Joe Mankiewicz was always a better writer than director. John Huston was a brilliant, perhaps great, director who also wrote well. It's hard to tell about directors whose language I can't speak. I'll never forget my shock at *Zabriskie Point,* Antonioni's first picture in English. I had always loved his work. I still loved what he'd done directorially, but the language in the picture was a real problem.

Most writers who began directing did so in order to protect the integrity of their work. They'd been violated so many times by directors who had no idea what they were doing that the writers picked up the megaphone in self-defense. I have written two scripts (*Prince of the City,* in collaboration with Jay Presson Allen, and *Q & A*), because I was particularly close to the stories and felt I knew the "sound" of the characters as well as anyone. That said, I consider myself a director, not a writer. There's a powerful magic about being a writer that I still marvel at.

Finally, I must confess that the closeness expressed for writers might be a bit disingenuous on my part. There are times when writers are a pain in the ass. (I'm sure any number of writers have felt the same about me.) Sometimes they have taken the job as a gig to earn a buck (as I have), to work rather than not work (as I also have). I'm pretty sure that if I want a new writer on the script, the studio or producer will let me pick one. But I've only done this once. Final cut is a tremendous source of security: I can eliminate a scene or a line that I don't like or haven't liked from the beginning. This has happened more than once. But not often. The director, because he says "Print," has a lot of power. But the results are best when he doesn't have to use it.

3

STYLE
The Most Misused Word Since Love

Not so long ago, I read a review of *Carlito's Way*, directed by Brian De Palma. The critic was an admirer of his work, as I am. The critic wrote that De Palma had found an ideal visual style for tragedy. However, there's a problem here. *Carlito's Way* is not a tragedy. In the same review, the critic wrote that the picture was "a conventional genre piece," adding that "there's really no way to think of this picture as a unified coherent work" and calling the picture "coarse, commercial material."

If De Palma found "the ideal visual technique to express the straight-line inexorability of tragedy" in the movie that is described in the earlier quotes, what would he have to find to bring *Oedipus Rex* or *Hamlet* to the screen?

My quarrel is not with De Palma or even with the picture, but with the critic.

Discussions of style as something totally detached from the content of the movie drive me mad. Form *does* follow function—in movies too. I realize there are many works of art that are so beautiful they need no justification. And maybe some movies wanted nothing *but* to be beautiful, or to be just a visual exercise or experiment. And the results might be highly emotional *because* they were only supposed to be beautiful. But let's not start using highfalutin terms like "ideal visual technique of tragedy."

Making a movie has always been about telling a story. Some movies tell a story and leave you with a feeling. Some tell a story and leave you with a feeling and give you an idea. Some tell a story, leave you with a feeling, give you an idea, and reveal something about yourself and others. And surely the *way* you tell that story should relate somehow to what that story is.

Because that's what style is: the way you tell a particular story. After the first critical decision ("What's this story about?") comes the second most important decision: "Now that I know *what* it's about, *how* shall I tell it?" And this decision will affect every department involved in the movie that is about to be made.

Let me vent my anger first, so it's out of the way. Critics talk about style as something apart from the movie because they need the style to be obvious. The reason they need it to be obvious is that they don't really *see*. If the movie looks like a Ford or Coca-Cola commercial, they think that's style. And it is. It's trying to sell you something you don't need and is stylistically geared to that goal. As soon as a "long lens" appears, that's "style." (A long lens photographs objects or people that are very far away and brings them up very close. But its focus is so shallow that everything in front of or behind the person or object is so blurred as to be unrecognizable. More on lenses later.) From the huzzahs that greeted Lelouch's *A Man and a Woman*, one would've thought that another Jean Renoir had arrived. A perfectly pleasant bit of romantic fluff was proclaimed "art," because it was so easy to identify as something other than realism. It's not so hard to see the style in *Murder on the Orient Express.* But almost no critic spotted the stylization in *Prince of the City.* It's one of the most stylized movies I've ever made. Kurosawa spotted it, though. In one of the most thrilling moments of my professional life, he talked to me about the "beauty" of the camera work as well as of the picture. But he meant beauty in the sense of its organic connection to the material. And this is the connection that, for me, separates true stylists from decorators. The decorators are easy to recognize. That's why critics love them so. There! I've had my tantrum.

This, of course, brings up the auteur argument. So-and-so's "style" is present in all his pictures. Of course it is. He directed them. One of the reasons Hitchcock was so deservedly adored was that his personal style was strongly felt in every picture. But it's important to realize why: He always essentially made the same picture. The stories weren't the same, but the genre was: a melodrama, layered with light comedy, played by the most glamorous actors he could find (also the most commercially popular at the time), photographed often by the same cameraman, with music composed by the same composer. The Hitchcock team was available for every picture. You're damn right there was a readily identifiable style. His *how* to do it was the same because *what* he was doing was the same. This is by no means a criticism. I've had more joy watching his pictures than those of many so-called serious directors. I'm only saying that with Hitchcock, form also followed function. Or perhaps it was the reverse. Perhaps he chose subjects that played into his strength, what he knew was his "style."

Then we arrive at the next ill-considered theory. "What

about Matisse? You can always recognize a Matisse." Of course you can. It's the work of one person *working alone!* Movie directors do *not* work alone. There will be a visual difference if we work with Cameraman A or Cameraman B, Production Designer C or Production Designer D. I've tried to work in as many genres as possible. I have cast cameramen or composers the same way I have actors: Are they right for this picture? Boris Kaufman, with whom I did eight pictures, was a great dramatic cameraman. We made wonderful movies together: *12 Angry Men, The Pawnbroker, The Fugitive Kind.* But when a lighter touch was needed, we ran into problems. A silly little romance we did, *That Kind of Woman,* failed visually; *The Group* and *Bye Bye Braverman* both suffered because photographically they were too heavy. Boris couldn't lighten up, literally. (There were reasons for his heavy heart.) And the movies he was right for, including *On the Waterfront* and *Baby Doll,* are among the finest black-and-white pictures ever made.

I've worked with the same cameraman on my last ten pictures, Andrzej Bartkowiak, because his range is incredibly broad. But on my secret list I have four or five other cameramen I want to work with in case I ever get certain scripts made. And as varied as his work has been with me, Andrzej's work took on an entirely different dimension when he worked so wonderfully with John Huston on *Prizzi's Honor* or Joel Schumacher on *Falling Down.*

Good style, to me, is unseen style. It is style that is felt. The style of Kurosawa's *Ran* is totally different from the style of *The Seven Samurai* or *Kurosawa's Dreams.* And yet they are certainly Kurosawa's movies. Stylistically, *Apocalypse Now* and *The Godfather* I and II have nothing in common. Yet all are clearly the work of Francis Ford Coppola. One source of the great visual differences in these movies is the cameraman. Gordon Willis shot both *Godfathers* and Vittorio Storaro *Apocalypse Now.*

Any movie is by definition an artificial creation. It's made by people coming together to explore a story. Stories take various forms. There are four primary forms of storytelling—tragedy, drama, comedy, and farce. No category is absolute. In *City Lights,* Chaplin moves from one form to the other with such grace that you're never aware of which of them you're in. Furthermore, there are subdivisions in drama and comedy. In drama, there is naturalism *(Dog Day Afternoon)* and realism *(Serpico).* In comedy, there is high comedy *(The Philadelphia Story)* and low comedy *(Abbott and Costello Meet You Name It).* Some pictures deliberately contain more than one form. *The Grapes of Wrath* is a combination of realism and tragedy, *Blazing Saddles* a combination of low comedy and farce. These are not exact, quantifiable elements, and very often they overlap. What I always try to determine is the general area where I think the picture belongs, because the first step in finding the style is to start narrowing down the choices I'll have to make.

As this paring down starts, an interesting phenomenon begins to take place. Clearly, the production starts to become more stylized. The increased stylization can reveal a more profound truth. Carl Dreyer's *The Passion of Joan of Arc* is a perfect example. The picture was made within a very limited (highly stylized) vocabulary. As the range of visual language was reduced, the movie took on wider and wider implications. Finally, a simple close-up of Falconetti in Joan's last moment of suffering said it all: war, death, religion, transcendence.

The more confined and specific the choices were, the more universal the results became.

To go literally from the sublime to the ridiculous, Hollywood usually thinks that universality means generalization. Many years ago I wanted very much to direct the movie of *Marjorie Morningstar.* It was a world I knew well, I adored the script, and, primarily because it involved Jewish middle-class life in New York, I was afraid for the Jews if I *didn't* do it. So one morning I flew out to California for a meeting with Jack Warner. As I came into his office, I saw scenic sketches of the Catskill Mountain Jewish resort where much of the action took place. Dick Sylbert, the production designer, was there. We'd worked together often. The sketches looked as if the whole resort was somewhere in Beverly Hills or Brentwood. I told Dick I'd never seen a borscht circuit camp that looked like that. Dick said, "Well, if you want it to look real . . . ," and he trailed off. At this point Jack Warner jumped in. "You see, Sidney," he said, "we don't want a picture with a narrow appeal. We want something more universal." I said, "That means we don't cast any Jews, right?" I was on the three o'clock plane home.

For me, coming down to the style of the movie happens in one of three ways. Sometimes it's through a process of elimination: Well, it's not this . . . it's not that. . . . This was true of *Prince of the City,* for example. As I've said, the *what* of this picture was: In a world of secrets, nothing is what it seems. I'll discuss in later chapters how this affected the camera, the sets and costumes, the editing, etc., but to begin with, that theme eliminated certain stylistic choices. Even though it was a true story, it was not going to be a naturalistic film. By naturalistic, I mean as close to documentary filmmaking as one can get in a scripted movie. This was not a conventionally structured story, in which the leading character goes from A to B to C, emerging triumphant or defeated in absolute terms. In fact, its ambiguity on every level was one of the most exciting things about it. I didn't even know how *I* felt about the leading character: was he a hero or a villain? I never did find out until I saw the completed picture. The good guys were bad guys a lot of the time, and vice versa. It wasn't a fictional story, and yet its moral issues were of a size that few real-life incidents attain. I wasn't sure whether we were in drama or tragedy territory. I knew I wanted to wind up somewhere between the two, leaning toward the tragic. Tragedy, when it works, leaves no room for tears. Tears would have been too easy in that movie. The classic definition of tragedy still works: pity and terror or awe, arriving at catharsis. That sense of awe requires a certain distance. It's hard to be in awe of someone you know well. The first thing affected was casting. If the leading role of Danny Ciello was played by De Niro or Pacino, all ambivalence would disappear. By their nature, stars invite your faculty of identification. You empathize with them immediately, even if they're playing monsters. A major star would defeat the picture with just the advertising. I chose a superb but not very well known actor, Treat Williams. This may have defeated the commerciality of the movie, but it was the right choice dramatically. Then I went further. I cast as many new faces as possible. If the actor had done lots of movies, I didn't use him. In fact, for the first time in one of my pictures, out of 125 speaking parts, I cast 52 of them from "civilians"—people who had never acted before. This helped enormously in two areas: first, in distancing the audience by not giving them actors with whom they had associations; and second, in giving the picture a disguised "naturalism," which would be slowly eroded as the picture wore on.

On a true tragedy, *Long Day's Journey Into Night,* I took the opposite tack. We had to achieve in the production the tragic dimensions of the script. I wanted not just stars but *giants.* They had to be the best actors—great actors, if possible—and, in addition, have great personas. I thought immediately of Katharine Hepburn for the critical role of Mary Tyrone. My first meeting with Hepburn did not go well. (More later.) I felt she was fighting to dominate the situation, which could lead to problems during shooting. When we left the meeting, Ely Landau, the producer, asked if I wanted to look for someone else. "No," I said. "She's magnificent. When Mary Tyrone falls, it's got to be like a giant oak falling. I'll work through whatever problems arise. Let's go with her." Ralph Richardson and Jason Robards also had powerful personalities supporting their brilliant talent. Dean Stockwell's part is poorly written, but visually he was the embodiment of the tortured young poet. And that was the cast.

Sometimes the style of the picture is apparent when I close the script after the first reading. That's the second—and easiest—way of deciding on a style. *Murder on the Orient Express* is one example. There we were dealing with a melodrama that had a wonderful plot. But it also had to have another quality: romantic nostalgia. What could be more nostalgic or romantic than an all-star cast? This hadn't been done in years, though there had been any number of all-star casts in the thirties, forties, and fifties. The plot was wonderful but complicated. So what could make you listen more attentively than a "star" giving the clues? We wound up with Sean Connery, Ingrid Bergman, Lauren Bacall, Jacqueline Bisset, Vanessa Redgrave, John Gielgud, Michael York, Wendy Hiller, Albert Finney, Richard Widmark, Rachel Roberts, and Tony Perkins. Even the supporting parts were treated as larger than life. For the small part of the doctor, I chose George Coulouris. A lovely actor, he nevertheless pours ten quarts of water into a five-quart pail when he acts. Perfect. The stars helped make the implausible plausible.

Another example of knowing immediately was *Dog Day Afternoon*. Because of the then shocking material, I felt that my first obligation was to let the audience know this really had happened. That accounts for the whole opening section of the movie. We went out with a hidden camera and photographed every ordinary incident we could shoot on a hot August day. When we finally cut to Pacino, John Cazale, and Gary Springer sitting in a car in front of a bank, they seemed like just one more shot of a group of people on that oppressive summer day in New York. You weren't even aware that the story had begun.

The third way is a slow process of investigation where the style emerges from a constant reiteration of the theme. Long discussions with the writer, cameraman, production designer, and editor allow the style to, in a sense, "present itself." One day you suddenly know how to do the picture. This happened on *Daniel*. Theme: Who pays for the passions and commitments of the parents? The children, who never chose those passions and commitments. In addition, time was fractured. The script jumped forward and backward in time. Sometimes we were in the present, sometimes twenty years earlier, then five years earlier, then back to the present, then fifteen years earlier. What slowly "presented itself" was that if we visually separated the parents' lives from the children's, two worlds would emerge. We accomplished this through the use of color in the decor, filters in the camera, tempos in the editing. I'll break this down in later chapters. The essential thing, for now, is that a complex series of talks allowed us to find a solution that gave emotional weight to each character, resolved the story thematically, and, at the same time, let the audience know where they were in time.

There's so much more to say about style in movies. But I

have to leave that to the individual chapters that break down the visual and auditory components of a movie. Someone once asked me what making a movie was like. I said it was like making a mosaic. Each setup is like a tiny tile. You color it, shape it, polish it as best you can. You'll do six or seven hundred of these, maybe a thousand. (There can easily be that many set-ups in a movie.) Then you literally paste them together and hope it's what you set out to do. But if you expect the final mosaic to look like anything, you'd better know what you're going for as you work on each tiny tile.

When we're sitting at rushes, watching yesterday's work, the greatest compliment we can give each other is, "Good work. We're all making the same movie." That's style.

4

ACTORS
Can an Actor *Really* Be Shy?

Let's try to put aside all previous concepts of actors: cattle, dumb, spoiled, overpaid, oversexed, egotistical, temperamental, etc. Actors are a major part of any movie. Very often they're the reason you go to the movie. (I only wish the theater had stars with such loyal followings.) They are performing artists, and performing artists are complex people.

I love actors. I love them because they're brave. All good work requires self-revelation. A musician communicates feelings through the instrument he is playing, a dancer through body movement. The *talent* of acting is one in which the actor's thoughts and feelings are instantly communicated to the audience. In other words, the "instrument" that an actor is using is himself. It is *his* feelings, *his* physiognomy, *his* sexuality, *his* tears, *his* laughter, *his* anger, *his* romanticism, *his* tenderness, *his* viciousness, that are up there on the screen for all to see. That's not easy. In fact, quite often it's painful.

There are many actors who can duplicate life brilliantly. Every detail will be correct, beautifully observed and perfectly reproduced. One thing is missing, however. The character's not alive. I don't want life reproduced up there on the screen. I want life created. The difference lies in the degree of the actor's personal revelation.

I mentioned earlier how much I admire what Paul Newman has done with his life. He is an honorable man. He is also a very private man. We had worked together in television in the early fifties and done a brief scene together in a Martin Luther King documentary, so when we got together on *The Verdict,* we were immediately comfortable with each other. At the end of two weeks of rehearsal, I had a run-through of the script. (A run-through is a rehearsal that goes straight through the entire script, with no stops between scenes.) There were no major problems. In fact, it seemed quite good. But somehow it seemed rather flat. When we broke for the day, I asked Paul to stay a moment. I told him that while things looked promising, we really hadn't hit the emotional level we both knew was there in David Mamet's screenplay. I said that his characterization was fine but hadn't yet evolved into a living, breathing person. Was there a problem? Paul said that he didn't have the lines memorized yet and that when he did, it would all flow better. I told him I didn't think it was the lines. I said that there was a certain aspect of Frank Galvin's character that was missing so far. I told him that I wouldn't invade his privacy, but only he could choose whether or not to reveal that part of the character and therefore that aspect of himself. I couldn't help him with the decision. We lived near each other and rode home together. The ride that evening was silent. Paul was thinking. On Monday, Paul came in to rehearsal and sparks flew. He was superb. His character and the picture took on life.

I know that decision to reveal the part of himself that the character required was painful for him. But he's a dedicated actor as well as a dedicated man. And, to answer the chapter heading, yes, Paul *is* a shy man. And a wonderful actor. And race car driver. And gorgeous.

If that personal revelation was as painful as it was for Paul, try to imagine how painful it must be for actresses. They are not only asked to make the same degree of self-revelation but are, in addition, treated as sexual commodities. They may be asked to bare their breasts and/or bottoms or both. They know they'll have to lose ten pounds before shooting starts. They may have had collagen pumped into their lips, undergone liposuction to take fat out of their thighs, changed hair color and the shape of their eyebrows, had tucks behind the ears to tighten the skin around their necks. All this *before* they've even begun rehearsals. They've been accepted or rejected on a purely physical basis before anything about emotions or characterization even comes into play. It has to be humiliating. And to top it all off, they know that when they hit forty or forty-five, there will be fewer and fewer offers, and they won't be able to move into older parts the way men do. For forty-two-year-old Richard Gere to wind up with twenty-three-year-old Julia Roberts is perfectly acceptable. But just try the reverse.

I would've hated to leave Paul's decision until we were actually shooting the movie. It might have come out the same way, but maybe not. A much poorer picture would have resulted. It was the rehearsal period that gave us the time not only to prepare the mechanical aspects of the picture but to develop the closeness needed for private, emotional revelations.

I generally hold rehearsals for a period of two weeks. Depending on the complexity of the characters, we sometimes work longer—four weeks on *Long Day's Journey Into Night*, three weeks on *The Verdict*.

Generally, we'll spend the first two or three days around a table, talking about the script. The first thing to be established is, of course, the theme. Then we're into each character, each scene, each line. It's much the same as the time I've spent with the writer. I'll have all the leading actors in on rehearsal. Sometimes an actor will have a critical scene with a character who appears in only one scene in the movie. I'll bring that small-part actor in for a day or two in the second week of rehearsals. We read the script nonstop first, then spend the next two days breaking it down into its components, winding up on the third day with another nonstop reading.

One of the interesting peculiarities in the process is that the second nonstop reading, after three days of rehearsal, usually isn't as good as the first. This is because the actors' instincts were pushing them on that first day. But instinct wears out quickly in acting, because of repetition. The nature of moviemaking is repetition. So one has to substitute "actions" that can stimulate emotions to compensate for the loss of instinct. That's what the two days of discussions have been about. In other words, we've begun to use technique. By the time we reach that second reading, instinct has been used up, but we still haven't had enough time to find all the emotional triggers that the actors need. And this is why the reading isn't as good.

In this same period we're seeing if any rewrites are necessary. We're beginning to sense whether transitions are missing in character or plot, whether all the necessary information is conveyed clearly, whether the picture is too long or its dialogue not crisp enough. If there's major work to be done, the writer may disappear for a few days. Minor revisions can be handled right in the rehearsal hall.

On the fourth day, I start blocking (that is, staging) the scenes. Each interior we'll use in the movie has been laid out in tape on the floor in its actual dimensions. The tapes are in different colors, so everyone can see which rooms they represent. Furniture is put in the same places where it will appear on the actual sets. Phones, desks, beds, knives, guns, handcuffs, pens, books, papers—all there. Two chairs, side by side, become a car, six chairs a subway. The actors are up on their feet, and it's "Cross here," "Sit on this line," "Sidney, I'd be more comfortable not looking at her in this section." We stage everything: chases, fights (knee, elbow, and hip pads a must), walks in Central Park, everything, whether indoors or out. I call it "throwing it up on its feet." The process takes about two and a half days.

Then we start again from the beginning, stopping now to make sure every move in the staging flows from what was discussed around the table. I don't stage the piece in my head before rehearsals. Nor have I laid out much in the way of camera movement. I want to see where the actors' instincts lead them. I want each step to flow organically from the previous step: from reading to staging to deciding how to shoot the picture. This stop-and-go, on-our-feet procedure may take another two and a half days. So by now we're in our ninth day. I'll ask the cameraman in to watch a run-through. The writer has been in attendance throughout. And if I like the producer, I'll invite him to the camera run-through.

On the final day of rehearsal, we'll do one or two run-throughs. Of course, I always rehearse in sequence. This is because movies are never shot in sequence. Access to locations, budget, the availability of actors playing smaller parts, proximity of locations so the trucks don't have too far to travel—many different priorities exist that force shooting to be scheduled in a certain way. Rehearsing in sequence gives the actors the sense of continuity, the "arc" of their characters, so they know exactly where they are when shooting begins, regardless of the shooting order.

Howard Hawks was once asked to name the most important element in an actor's performance. His answer was "confidence." In a sense, that is really what's been going on during rehearsal: the actors are gaining confidence in revealing their inner selves. They've been learning about me. I hold nothing back. If the actors are going to hold nothing back in front of the camera, I can hold nothing back in front of them. They have to be able to trust me, to know that I "feel" them and what they're doing. This mutual trust is the most important element between the actor and me.

I worked with Marlon Brando on *The Fugitive Kind*. He's a suspicious fellow. I don't know if he bothers anymore, but Brando tests the director on the first or second day of shooting. What he does is to give you two apparently identical takes. Except that on one, he is really working from the inside; and on the other, he's just giving you an *indication* of what the emotion was like. Then he watches which one you decide to print. If the director prints the wrong one, the "indicated" one, he's had it. Marlon will either walk through the rest of the performance or make the director's life hell, or both. Nobody has the right to test people like that, but I can understand why he does that. He doesn't want to pour out his inner life to someone who can't see what he's doing.

At the same time they're learning about me, I'm finding out things about the actors. What stimulates them, what triggers their emotions? What annoys them? How's their concentration? Do they have a technique? What method of acting do they use? The "Method" made famous at the Actors' Studio, based on the teaching of Stanislavsky, is not the *only* one. Ralph Richardson, whom I saw give at least three *great* performances, in theater and film, used a completely auditory, musical system. During rehearsals of *Long Day's Journey Into Night,* he asked a simple question. Forty-five minutes later I finished my answer. (I talk a lot.) Ralph paused a moment and then sonorously said, "I see what you mean, dear boy: a little more cello, a little less flute." I was, of course, enchanted. And of course he was putting me down, telling me not to be so long-winded. But we talked in musical terms from then on: "Ralph, a little more staccato." "A slower tempo, Ralph." I subsequently found out that when he appeared in the theater, he played a violin in his dressing room before a performance as a warm-up. He used himself as a musical instrument, literally.

Other actors work in rhythms: "Sidney, give me the rhythm of it." The answer is "Dum-de-dum-de-dum-de-DUM." Or they want line readings, a technique other actors hate.

The actors are also learning about each other. They are revealing themselves *to* each other, sharing, in greater and greater amounts, their personal feelings. Henry Fonda told me that on the first day of shooting a Sergio Leone movie, he had to shoot a sexy love scene with Gina Lollobrigida. No rehearsal. Right to it. Actors are very different about love and sex scenes. Some shy away from them. The wife of an actor I worked with wouldn't allow him to do them. I know that if an affair develops between two actors, it will usually begin on either the day I stage the love scene or the day I shoot it. An actor who must remain nameless wanted to be in on the casting of the woman who was going to play opposite him. When I asked why, he said he had to be able to relate to her sexually if he was to play the love scenes properly. So I asked him, what if the script called for him to kill her? Would he have to relate to her murderously in order to play the part? Things were a little testy between us for the next few days.

The most moving example of how much of themselves actors must pour into a character happened on *Network*. William Holden was a wonderful actor. He was also very experienced. He'd done sixty or seventy movies by the time we worked together, maybe more. I noticed that during the rehearsal of one particular scene with Faye Dunaway, he looked everywhere but directly into her eyes. He looked at her eyebrows, her hair, her lips, but not her eyes. I didn't say anything. The scene was a confession by his character that he was hopelessly in love with her, that they came from very different worlds, that he was achingly vulnerable to her and therefore needed her help and support. On the day of shooting we did a take. After the take, I said, "Let's go again, and Bill, on this take, would you try something for me? Lock into her eyes and never break away from them." He did. Emotion came pouring out of him. It's one of his best scenes in the movie. Whatever he'd been avoiding could no longer be denied. The rehearsal period had helped me recognize this emotional reticence in him.

Of course, I never asked him what he had been avoiding. The actor has a right to his privacy; I never violate his private sources knowingly. Some directors do. There's no right or wrong here. But I had learned my lesson many years earlier, on a picture called *That Kind of Woman*. I needed tears from an actor on a particular line. She couldn't do it. Finally, I told her that no matter what I did during the next take, she should keep going and say the line. We rolled the camera. Just before she reached the line, I hauled off and slapped her. Her eyes widened. She looked stunned. Tears welled up, overflowed, she said the line, and we had a terrific take. When I called,

"Cut, print!" She threw her arms around me, kissed me, and told me I was brilliant. But I was sick with self-loathing. I ordered an ice pack so her cheek wouldn't swell up and knew that I would never do anything like that again. If we can't get it by craftsmanship, to hell with it. We'll find something else that'll work as well.

In the chapter on style, I mentioned that for *Long Day's Journey Into Night* I wanted Katharine Hepburn because of her acting and her strong persona. The problem of integrating the very strong personal qualities with the character the star is playing is a fascinating one. If you've got a major star, you've got that strong personal quality seeping through in every performance. Even with as fine a character actor as Robert De Niro, De Niro himself comes out. Partially it's because he uses himself brilliantly. As I said earlier, the actor's only instrument is himself. But I think it's more than that. There's a mysterious alchemy between star and audience. Sometimes it's based on the physical beauty or sex appeal of the star. But I don't believe that it's ever just one thing. Surely there were other women as attractive as Marilyn Monroe or men as handsome as Cary Grant (though not many). Al Pacino tries to suit his looks to the characters—a beard here, long hair there—but somehow it's the way his eyes express an enormous rage, even in tender moments, that enthralls me and everyone else. I think that every star evokes a sense of danger, something unmanageable. Perhaps each person in the audience feels that he or she is the one who can manage, tame, satisfy the bigger-than-life quality that a star has. Clint Eastwood isn't really the same as you or me, is he? Or Michelle Pfeiffer, or Sean Connery, or you name them. I don't really know what makes a star. But the persona that jumps out at you is certainly a most important element.

Because they are often the reason that a picture gets financed, actors tend to get spoiled. I hate those large trailers. I've seen trailers that are literally converted buses. The bed is enormous. The TV has a retractable satellite dish. I've seen the production company pay for private cooks, private secretaries, makeup and hair people who are no better than their peers but draw four times the salary. Many of the stars' makeup and hair people engage in a subtle kind of undermining, so that the star slowly becomes dependent on them. All of this is dangerous in two ways: it costs a lot of money that doesn't wind up on the screen; and even without meaning to, the stars begin to get a sense of power that can hurt their work.

Hepburn would never stoop to that level. She had, however, been a dominant factor in her own career. This was during her time at Metro, in the thirties and forties. Most stars were in abject fear of Louis B. Mayer, but not Kate. She sometimes created her own material. I don't know if she commissioned Philip Barry to write *The Philadelphia Story* for her, but she owned the rights. When we first met, on *Long Day's Journey,* she was living in John Barrymore's former house in Los Angeles. I stepped through the doors of what seemed to me a fifty-foot living room. She stood at the opposite end of the room and started toward me. We'd covered about half the distance when she said, "When do you want to start rehearsal?" (No "Hello" or "How do you do?") "September nineteenth," I said. "I can't start till the twenty-sixth," she said. "Why?" I asked. "Because then," she said, "you'd know more about the script than I would."

Funny, charming, but she meant it. It was perfectly all right with me if she knew more about the character. After all, she was going to play it, and I had a lot of other things to think about. But the challenge was unmistakable, and I could see trouble down the road.

The solution was to leave her alone. Though she had played great roles, nothing could compare with Mary Tyrone for psychological complexity, physical and emotional demand, and tragic dimension. During the first three days of rehearsal I said nothing to her about Mary Tyrone's character. I talked at length with Jason, who'd played his part before, with Ralph and Dean, and of course we talked about the play. When we finished the run-through reading on the third day, there was a long pause. And then, from Kate's corner of the table, a small voice called out, "Help!"

From then on, the work was thrilling. She asked, she told, she fretted, she tried, she failed, she won. She built that character stone by stone. Something was still tight about the performance until the end of the second week. There's a moment in the script when her youngest son, trying to cut through her morphine haze, screams at her that he's dying of consumption. I said, "Kate, I'd like you to haul off and smack him as hard as you can." She started to say that she couldn't do that, but the sentence died halfway out of her mouth. She thought about it for thirty seconds, then said, "Let's try it." She hit him. She looked at Dean's horrified face, and her shoulders started to shake. She dissolved into the broken, frightened failure that was so important an aspect of Mary Tyrone. The sight of that giant Hepburn in such a state was the personification of tragic acting. When the Greeks said tragedy is for royalty, they were only saying that tragedy was for giants. There was no tightness ever again. Kate was soaring.

At the end of rehearsal, just before shooting, I gathered the actors to tell them about my shooting system and habits and to find out if there was anything they needed during shooting that we could provide. At this session, I said to them, "And by the way, you're all invited to rushes." As we were leaving, Kate called me aside. "Sidney," she said, "I've gone to rushes of practically every picture I've ever made. But I won't be coming to these rushes. I can see how you work. I know Boris's work. [Boris Kaufman was the cameraman.] You're both dead honest. You can't protect me. If I go to rushes, all that I'll see is this"—and she reached under her chin and pinched the slightly sagging flesh—"and this"—she did the same thing under her arms—"and I need all my strength and concentration to just play the part." Tears sprang to my eyes. I'd never seen an actor with such self-knowledge and such dedication, trust, and bravery. She was breaking habits of thirty years because she knew they would interfere with the job. *That's* a giant.

In *Murder on the Orient Express,* I wanted Ingrid Bergman to play the Russian Princess Dragomiroff. She wanted to play the retarded Swedish maid. I wanted Ingrid Bergman. I let her play the maid. She won an Academy Award. I bring this up because self-knowledge is important in so many ways to an actor. Earlier, I mentioned how improvisation can be an effective tool in rehearsal as a way of finding out what you're really like when, for example, you're angry. Knowing your feelings lets you know when those feelings are real as opposed to when you're simulating them. No matter how insecure, almost all the stars I've worked with have a high degree of self-knowledge. They may hate what they see, but they do see themselves. And you thought all that gazing into the mirror was just vanity. I think it's self-knowledge that serves as the integrating element between the actor's natural persona and the character he's playing.

We're fortunate in this country. Almost all our stars are very good actors. And of the ones who aren't, most of them want to be. So a great many study acting when they're not working. Many attend classes of different kinds on both coasts. In London too, different techniques are taught. How does Paul Newman (the Method) work with Charlotte Rampling (no method, but wonderful); Alan King (nightclubs) with Ali Mac-Graw (no formal training); Ralph Richardson (classical Royal Academy) with Dean Stockwell (a version of the Method); Marlon Brando (the Method) with Anna Magnani (self-taught)? How can we get actors with totally different life experiences and acting techniques to look like they're making the same movie?

The answer is remarkably simple, but like all simple things, it's hard to achieve. Just as in life, really talking and listening to one another is very, very difficult. In acting, that's the basis on which everything is built. By now I have an almost set speech I make just before the first reading of the script. I will say to the actors, "Go as far as you feel. Do as much or as little as you want to. If you feel it, let it fly. Don't worry whether it's the right emotion or the wrong one. We'll find out. That's what rehearsals are for. But minimally, *talk to each other and listen to each other.* Don't worry about losing your place in the script as long as you're really talking and listening to each other. Try to pick up on what you just heard." Sanford Meisner was one of the best acting teachers of my time. With beginning students, he spent the first month or six weeks getting them to really talk and listen to one another. That's all. It's the great common denominator where different acting styles and techniques meet.

A charming thing happened at the first reading of *Murder on the Orient Express.* Five stars of the English theater were appearing in the West End at the time—John Gielgud, Wendy Hiller, Vanessa Redgrave, Colin Blakely, and Rachel Roberts. Sitting with them were six movie stars: Sean Connery, Lauren Bacall, Richard Widmark, Tony Perkins, Jacqueline Bisset, and Michael York; Ingrid Bergman and Albert Finney bridged both worlds. They began to read. I couldn't hear anything. Everyone was murmuring their lines so quietly they were inaudible. I finally figured out what was happening. The movie stars were in awe of the theater stars; the theater stars were in awe of the movie stars. A classic case of stage fright. I stopped the reading and, saying that I couldn't hear a thing, asked them to please talk to one another as if we were at Gielgud's house for dinner. John said he'd never *had* such illustrious guests to dinner, and off we went.

Most good actors have their best take early. Usually, by the fourth time you've done it (Take 4), they've poured out the best in themselves. This is particularly true of big, emotional scenes. Movies, however, are a technical medium. Things go wrong despite preparations. A door slams off the set, the microphone gets in the shot, the camera operator goofs, the dolly pusher misses his cue. When this happens, the actor has an awful time. Having "emptied out" once, he now has to fill up again. The only way around the problem is to shoot take after take, because the "refill" can come at any time after Take 8 or Take 10 or Take 12. I try to supply the actor with something new each time to stimulate his feelings, but after a time my imagination runs out.

One story sums up all the painful problems I've been talking about in this chapter. It was on *The Fugitive Kind.* In a scene with Anna Magnani, Brando had a long speech that contained some of Tennessee Williams's best writing. Using beautiful imagery, he compares himself to a bird that's never able to find itself at home anywhere on earth. Condemned to soar aimlessly over the world, it never alights until it dies. Boris Kaufman had arranged some complex lighting changes. The light on the back walls slowly faded away until only Marlon was left lit, in a kind of limbo. A complicated camera move was also part of the shot.

Marlon started Take 1. About two-thirds of the way through the speech, he stopped. He'd forgotten his lines. We started Take 2. The lights didn't fade properly. Take 3: Marlon forgot his lines at the exact same spot. Take 4: Marlon stopped again at the same line. Until then, I had never gone more than four takes with Marlon on anything. Take 5: The camera move was wrong. Take 6. Take 7. Take 8. Marlon's memory was failing at *the same line.* By now it was 5:30. We were on overtime. Marlon had told me about some personal problems he was having at the time. I suddenly realized there was a direct connection between his troubles and the line he couldn't remember. We tried again. He stopped. I went up to him and said that if he wanted, we could break until tomorrow, but I didn't want this block to build up overnight. I thought we should bull through it no matter how long it took. Marlon agreed. Take 12. Take 18. It was getting embarrassing. Magnani, the crew, all of us were in agony for him. Take 22. No good for camera. It was almost a relief when something was *not* Marlon's fault. I debated whether to say anything about what I thought was bothering him. I decided it would be too great a personal violation of a confidence. Take 27, 28. I told Marlon that since I'd be cutting to Anna anyway, we could do a pickup. A pickup is where you begin a new take at the point where the old take was interrupted. Marlon said no. He wanted to get it all in one take. The ending of the speech would be stronger that way.

Finally, on Take 34, two and a half hours after we started, he did it all. And beautifully. I almost wept with relief. We walked back to his dressing room together. Once we were inside, I told him that I might have been able to help him but felt it wasn't my right. He looked at me and smiled as only Brando can smile, so that you think daybreak has come. "I'm glad you didn't," he said. We hugged and went home.

Everything about actors and movie acting is in that story. The use of self at whatever cost, the self-knowledge, the confidence that a director and actor have to develop in each other, the devotion to a text (Marlon never questioned the words), the dedication to the work, the craft.

It's experiences like that that make me love actors.

5

THE CAMERA
Your Best Friend

First of all, the camera can't talk back. It can't ask stupid questions. It can't ask penetrating questions that make you realize you've been wrong all along. Hey, it's a *camera!*

But:

- It can make up for a deficient performance.
- It can make a good performance better.
- It can create mood.
- It can create ugliness.
- It can create beauty.
- It can provide excitement.
- It can capture the essence of the moment.
- It can stop time.
- It can change space.
- It can define a character.
- It can provide exposition.

- It can make a joke.
- It can make a miracle.
- *It can tell a story!*

If my movie has two stars in it, I always know it really has three. The third star is the camera.

Mechanically, a camera's quite simple. A reel of unexposed negative is mounted on the front. A take-up reel, pulling the exposed negative and rolling it up, is on the back. In between are notched wheels that keep the film taut at all times. They turn at a constant rate of speed, passing through the perforations in the negative, so that during a take, the film is moving. In the center of this mechanism is a lens. The light comes through the lens and strikes the negative. The camera has actually photographed a still picture, called a frame. After the frame is exposed, the camera's mechanism starts to pull the next frame into position behind the lens. But as the film moves, a shutter comes down and blocks all light from hitting the negative. Then the next frame—another still photograph—is exposed. There are twenty-four frames per second, sixteen frames to a foot of film, one and one-half feet to twenty-four frames. When projected back onto a screen by exactly the same mechanism, it looks as if the images are in constant motion—even though we are actually seeing twenty-four still pictures per second. To the human eye, the movement looks continuous. As Jean-Luc Godard once said, movies "are twenty-four frames of truth per second." Like the fingering mechanisms of most musical instruments, this simple, clumsy contraption can produce a profound aesthetic result.

There are four primary elements that affect the picture produced in the camera. First, there is the light that exists even before it enters the lens. This light can be natural, artificial, or a combination of both. Second, there are color filters and nets, usually placed behind the lens, to control the color and change the quality of the light. Third, there is the size of the lens itself. Fourth is the lens stop, which determines the amount of light that will pass through the lens onto the film. There are other factors—the angle of the shutter, the negative stock, and so forth. But these four basic elements will suffice for now.

The most fundamental photographic choice I make is what lens to use for a particular shot. Lenses vary over an enormous range from 9 millimeters to 600 millimeters and beyond. Technically we refer to the lenses on the lower millimeter range (9 mm, 14 mm, 17 mm, 18 mm, 21 mm) as wide-angle lenses, and to those from 75 mm on up as long lenses. I hope I can help make this clear with the following drawings:

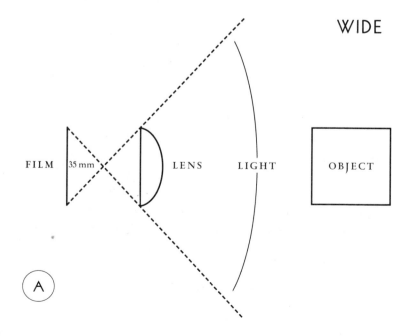

LONG

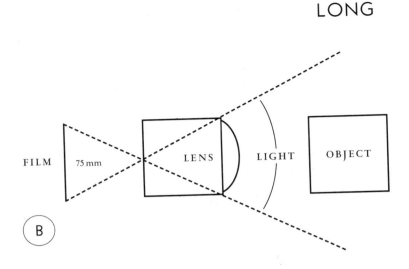

The distance from where the image reverses itself to the recording surface (the film) is what determines the millimeter count of the lens. In drawing A, notice how much more room there is above and below the photographed object than in drawing B. The 35 mm lens (A) takes in a significantly larger area than the 75 mm lens (B). The wider-angle lens (35 mm) has a much larger "field" than the 75 mm lens. The 75 mm lens has a long tube drawn on it because it needs more distance from the recording surface. Theoretically, given all the space one needed, one could achieve the same size of any photographed object using a longer lens by simply backing the camera up. But changing lenses for the amount of information the lens gathers (its "field") is only a partial use of a lens. Lenses have different *feelings* about them. *Different lenses will tell a story differently.*

Murder on the Orient Express illustrated this very clearly. During the body of the picture, various scenes took place that would be retold at the end of the movie by Hercule Poirot, our genius detective, using the retelling as part of his evidence in the solution of the crime. While he described the incidents, the scenes we'd seen earlier were repeated as flashbacks. Only now, because they'd taken on a greater melodramatic significance as evidence, they appeared on the screen much more dramatically, forcefully, etched in hard lines. This was accomplished through the use of different lenses. Each scene that would be repeated was shot twice—the first time with normal lenses for the movie (50 mm, 75 mm, 100 mm) and the second time with a very wide-angle lens (21 mm). The result was that the first time we saw the scene, it appeared as a normal part of the movie. Viewed the second time, it was melodramatic, fitting in with the drama of a solution to a murder.

Lenses have different characteristics. No lens truly sees what the human eye sees, but the lenses that come closest are the midrange lenses, from 28 mm to 40 mm. Wide-angle lenses (9 mm to 24 mm) tend to distort the picture; the wider the lens, the greater the distortion. The distortions are spatial. Objects seem farther apart, especially objects lined up from foreground to background. Vertical lines seem to be forced closer together at the top of the frame.

Longer lenses (from 50 mm upward) compress the space. Objects that are lined up from foreground to background seem closer together. The longer the lens, the closer the objects seem, both to the camera and to one another. These distortions are tremendously useful. For example, if I were doing a tracking shot or dolly, or simply panning from right to left, I could create the illusion of the photographed object traveling at much greater speed by using a long lens. Because it seems closer, the object seems to travel past the background at a much greater speed on a long lens. The foreground object (a car, a horse, a running person) *seems* to be covering more ground faster. Conversely, if I wanted to increase the speed of an object moving toward or away from me, I would use a wide-angle lens. This is because the object *seems* to be covering greater distances as it is approaching or leaving us.

The lenses have another characteristic. Wide-angle lenses have a much greater focal depth of field—the amount of space in which an object moving toward or away from the camera stays in focus without changing the focus of the lens mechanically. Again, this can be put to tremendous use. If I wanted to get rid of as much background as possible, I'd use a long lens. The background, even though it seems closer, is so out of focus that it becomes unrecognizable. But with a wide-angle lens, although the background seems farther away, it will be sharper and therefore more recognizable.

Sometimes, when I need a long lens but want to keep the image sharper, we'll pour in more light. The more light, the more focal depth, and vice versa. The added light will give us a greater focal depth, compensating somewhat for the loss of depth that the long lens created.

It gets even more complicated. Since light affects the focal depth, the stop (the amount of light allowed to pass through the lens) is very important. The stop is created by opening or closing a diaphragm mounted in the lens. We call it opening up (letting in more light by setting the diaphragm in its most open position) or stopping down (closing the diaphragm so it allows the least amount of light to reach the film). Whew!

The purpose of these boring technical discussions is to convey that the basic photographic elements—lens, stop, light, and filters—are wonderful tools. They can be used not just out of necessity but to achieve aesthetic results. Perhaps I can illustrate with some examples.

12 Angry Men, Boris Kaufman, photographer. It never occurred to me that shooting an entire picture in one room was a problem. In fact, I felt I could turn it into an advantage. One of the most important dramatic elements for me was the sense of entrapment those men must have felt in that room. Immediately, a "lens plot" occurred to me. As the picture unfolded, I wanted the room to seem smaller and smaller. That meant that I would slowly shift to longer lenses as the picture continued. Starting with the normal range (28 mm to 40 mm), we progressed to 50 mm, 75 mm, and 100 mm lenses. In addition, I shot the first third of the movie above eye level, and then, by lowering the camera, shot the second third at eye level, and the last third from below eye level. In that way, toward the end, the ceiling began to appear. Not only were the walls closing in, the ceiling was as well. The sense of increasing claustrophobia did a lot to raise the tension of the last part of the movie. On the final shot, an exterior that showed the jurors leaving the courtroom, I used a wide-angle lens, wider than any lens that had been used in the entire picture. I also raised the camera to the highest above-eye-level position. The intention was to literally give us all air, to let us finally breathe, after two increasingly confined hours.

The Fugitive Kind, Boris Kaufman, photographer. For the first time, I tried assigning lenses to characters. Brando's character, Val Xavier, is trying to find love for himself and others as the only possibility of his own salvation. (I once asked Tennessee

Williams if the name Val Xavier was a disguised version of St. Valentine, the savior. He merely smiled that enigmatic little smile of his.)

With a long lens, because of its shorter focal depth, the image tends to be a bit softer. In fact, by using a long lens at a wide-open stop, a close-up may have the eyes sharp but the ears and back of the head slightly out of focus. So I tried whenever possible to use a longer lens for Brando than for any other person in the scene. I wanted an aura around him of gentility and tenderness.

Anna Magnani's character, Lady, starts off as a hard, bitter woman. As her love affair with Val grows, she softens. So as the picture progressed, I slowly increased the use of long lenses on her until, toward the end, the same lens was used for Lady and Val. He'd changed her life. She was now in his world.

Val's character began and ended the same. Lady's character underwent a transition. To emphasize her progression, once we were using the same lens for each of them, we added nets to her side. A net is literally a piece of net held in a rigid metal frame that fits behind the lens, outside the camera. It diffuses the light, further softening the image. The net must be used very subtly, especially when it is intercut with shots of a character who does not have a net. There are various degrees of net, from light to heavy. At the end of the picture, Lady finds out she's pregnant. In a lovely speech, she compares herself to a fig tree in her father's garden that, once dead, came back to life. Boris used everything he could—long lens, nets, and three different stages of heavily gauzed light—to give her a glowing quality. Looking back on it now, I think we went a bit too far, but at the time I thought it looked great.

I'd like to pause here for a moment to talk about light. Clearly, there is more control on an interior, where the cameraman is providing the light artificially. But on exteriors, it's quite amazing to see how much control a good cameraman *does* have.

If you've ever passed a movie company shooting on the streets, you may have seen an enormous lamp pouring its light onto an actor's face. We call it an arc or a brute, and it gives off the equivalent of *12,000 watts.* Your reaction has probably been: What's the matter with these people? The sun's shining brightly and they're adding that big light so that the actor is practically squinting.

Well, film is limited in many ways. It's a chemical process, and one of its limitations is the amount of contrast it can take. It can adjust to a lot of light or a little bit of light. But it can't take a lot of light and a little bit of light in the same frame.

It's a poorer version of your own eyesight. I'm sure you've seen a person standing against a window with a bright, sunny day outside. The person becomes silhouetted against the sky. We can't make out his features. Those arc lamps correct the "balance" between the light on the actor's face and the bright sky. If we didn't use them, his face would go completely black. And an arc does cause squinting. (I'll bet you thought all those Western heroes had that squint naturally.)

A perfect illustration of the use of contrast is:

The Hill, Oswald Morris, photographer. *The Hill* is the story of a British Army prison in North Africa during World War II. Only the camp is for *British* soldiers, sent there for discipline problems or criminal behavior. It's a brutal place, filled with sadistic punishments that are meant to break the spirit of anyone unlucky enough to be there. Wanting a very contrasty negative, we used Ilford stock, which was rarely used because photographers found it *too* contrasty.

We decided to shoot the entire picture on three wide lenses: the first third on a 24 mm, the second on a 21 mm, the last on an 18 mm. I mean everything, close-ups included. Of course, the faces became distorted. A nose looked twice as big, the forehead sloped backward. At the end, even on a close-up with the camera no more than a foot from the actors' faces, you could see the whole jail or enormous vistas of the desert behind them. That's why I used those lenses. I never wanted to lose the critical element in plot *and* emotion: these men were never going to be free of the jail or of themselves. That was the theme of the picture. I wanted their surroundings powerfully present at all times.

To get back to contrast, the exteriors were shot in the desert. The light was blinding, the heat so horrendous that during the day we dehydrated completely. After a few days I asked Sean Connery if he was peeing at all. "Only in the morning," he said.

When we came to a close-up and the actor wasn't facing the sun, Ossie would ask if I wanted to see the actor's face. If I said yes, the electricians would roll up the brute. If I said no, Ossie would say, "How about eyes?" If yes, he'd tear off a white piece of cardboard—or, if the camera was close enough to the actor, take his handkerchief—and use it as a reflector, to bounce the hot light from the sky into the actor's eyes.

In fact, in the early days of movies, before they had portable generators, cameramen used what were called reflectors— huge boards papered with silver foil, which would reflect the sun wherever the cameraman wanted. They are still used today when the budget is tight.

Murder on the Orient Express, Geoffrey Unsworth, photographer. Our goal here was sheer physical beauty. Two ways of achieving this (among many others) are the use of long lenses, to help soften the whole image, and backlight.

Backlight is one of the oldest and most frequently used ways of making people look more beautiful. Light is focused from behind the actor to the back of the head and shoulders. The light is of greater intensity than that hitting the actor's face. If you've ever walked in the woods toward a setting sun, or looked south down Fifth Avenue on a sunny day from a slightly elevated point of view, you might remember how beautiful the leaves or the avenue looked. That's because they were backlit. Backlight is used so much in movies because it works. It made Dietrich, Garbo, all of them, even more beautiful than they already were.

Network, Owen Roizman, photographer. The movie was about corruption. So we corrupted the camera. We started with an almost naturalistic look. For the first scene between Peter Finch and Bill Holden, on Sixth Avenue at night, we added only enough light to get an exposure. As the picture progressed, camera setups became more rigid, more formal. The lighting became more and more artificial. The next-to-final scene—where Faye Dunaway, Robert Duvall, and three network gray suits decide to kill Peter Finch—is lit like a commercial. The camera setups are static and framed like still pictures. The camera also had become a victim of television.

(All of these transitions in lenses and in lighting happen gradually. I don't like any technical devices to be apparent.

When they're stretched over a two-hour period, I don't think the audience is ever conscious of the changes taking place visually.)

The Deadly Affair, Freddie Young, photographer. Thematically it was a film about life's disappointments. I wanted to desaturate the colors. I wanted to get that dreary, lifeless feeling London has in winter. Freddie suggested preexposing the film. The film was taken into a darkroom *before* we used it in the camera and exposed very briefly to a sixty-watt bulb. The result was that the negative stock had a milky film over it. When it was exposed to the actual scene, almost all the colors were far less vibrant, with much less life and brightness than they normally would've had. This process is called "preflashing."

The Morning After, Andrzej Bartkowiak, photographer. Here I wanted the exact opposite of *The Deadly Affair.* Living in Los Angeles was part of the debilitating influence on the character played by Jane Fonda. I wanted all color exaggerated: reds redder, blues bluer. We used filters. Behind the lens are little slots where frames about two and a half inches by three and a half inches can be inserted. These frames and slots can hold pieces of glass or gelatin that are colored to various specifications. When we could see the sky, Andrzej would add a blue filter that covered only the sky. The sky came out bluer. Every color was reinforced in this way. One day, because of smog and clouds toward the end of the day, the sky had an orange haze. Andrzej turned the scene into the color of an Orange Julius hot dog stand.

These filters have some drawbacks. They limit camera

movement, since you don't want the blue sky filter to bleed into the white building or the actor's face. But used judiciously, they can be very helpful.

Colored gelatins can also be used in front of the lights that illuminate the set. Many photographers use them constantly. Oswald Morris, with whom I did three movies, began the technique with *Moulin Rouge,* where it was used for the entire film. The advantage of using gels on lights is that individual objects or parts of the set can be specifically colored as highlights or to define areas. Used over an entire set, they can convey a mood. Gels used on the lens cut down the amount of light and therefore affect the stop. Used in front of lights, the stop is unaffected or can be compensated for by more wattage.

Prince of the City, Andrzej Bartkowiak, photographer. Photographically, this was one of the most interesting pictures I've done. Going back to its theme (nothing is what it appears to be), I made a decision: We would not use the midrange lenses (28 mm through 40 mm). Nothing was to look normal, or anything close to what the eye would see. I took the theme literally. All space was elongated or foreshortened, depending on whether I used wide-angle or long lenses. A city block was twice as long or half as long, depending on the choice of lens. In addition, Andrzej and I laid out a very complex lighting plot. At the beginning of the movie, the leading character, Danny Ciello, was completely aware of everything around him. As events became more complex, as he lost more and more control over them, his moral crisis deepened. He knew he was being forced into a corner where he would have to betray his friends. His thoughts and actions became more focused on himself and his four police partners.

In the first third of the movie, we tried to have the light on the background brighter than on the actors in the foreground. For the second third, the foreground light and the background light were more or less balanced. For the last third, we cut the light off the background. Only the foreground, occupied by the actors, was lit. By the end of the movie, only the relationships that were about to be betrayed mattered. People emerged from the background. *Where* something took place no longer mattered. What mattered was *what* took place and to whom.

I made another decision that seems important to me. Except for one instance, I never framed a shot so the sky was visible. The sky meant freedom, release, but Danny had no way out. The only shot that had sky in the frame was practically nothing but sky. Danny is walking on the Manhattan Bridge. He climbs up a catwalk overlooking the rails of the subway that runs between Brooklyn and Manhattan. He is contemplating suicide. By now that's his only possible freedom, his only possible release.

Dog Day Afternoon, Victor Kemper, photographer. For this picture, I wanted the exact opposite of the rigid visual structure of *Prince of the City.*

As I said earlier, the first obligation was to let the audience know that this event had really happened. Therefore, the first decision made was that we use no artificial light. The bank was lit by fluorescents in the ceiling. If we had to supplement the light because of focus problems, we simply added more fluorescents. Outside, at night, all the light came from the enormous spotlights of the Police Emergency van on the scene. The bounce light reflecting off the white-brick-and-glass exterior of the bank was bright enough to illuminate the faces of the people facing the bank. Two blocks away, Victor placed a lamp to backlight the crowd standing on the corner. The lamp was placed above a real streetlight, and this gave the crowd a natural backlight. We had to augment it because the camera would not have been able to read the light on the crowd from the real streetlight. Inside the bank, when the power was shut off, the orange emergency lights automatically went on. We augmented these simply to get enough light for an exposure.

And for the improvised scenes in the street and in the bank, I used two and sometimes three hand-held cameras to reinforce the documentary feel.

Long Day's Journey Into Night, Boris Kaufman, photographer. A lot of critics condescendingly called it a "photographed stage play." This was easy to say, since I used the play's text. I even faded to black at act endings. The theatrical origin was easily identifiable. No effort was made to disguise it. But the critics were incapable of seeing one of the most complex camera and editing techniques of any picture I've done.

Obviously, I am very proud of it as a *movie.* Here's the main reason: If you took a close-up from Act I of Hepburn, Richardson, Robards, and Stockwell, put it into a slide projector, and next to it projected a close-up of those same people from Act IV, you'd be shocked at how different they look. The ravaged, worn, exhausted faces at the end have almost nothing to do with the composed, clean faces at the beginning. It wasn't only acting. This was also accomplished by lenses, light, camera position, and length of takes. (Editing and art direction will be dealt with later.)

At the start of the picture, everything was peachy-pie normal. Both the lenses and the light could have been used for an Andy Hardy movie. I moved the first part of Act I outdoors and shot it on a sunny day, so this journey into night could seem even longer. I wanted more light at the beginning to contrast with the blackness of the end.

As for interior light, each character was, whenever possible, lit differently—Hepburn and Stockwell always with gentle front light, Robards and Richardson with light centered but above them. As the picture continued, the light on the three men became harsher, more severe. This pattern was broken temporarily as Stockwell and Richardson went into their lyrical arias of self-examination in Act IV, when each one explores what he wanted in earlier and less tortured times. The light on Hepburn became softer, gentler, as the picture progressed.

Camera position was also important visually. For the men, we started at eye level and the camera slowly dropped, until in two critical scenes in Act IV, the camera was literally at floor level. For Hepburn, this pattern was reversed. Camera position went higher and higher until in her next-to-last scene at the end of Act III, I was using a crane to go higher still.

And, of course, lenses: longer and longer lenses on her as she slipped into her dope-ridden fog, wider and wider lenses on the men as their world crumbled around them.

In Act IV, there are two climactic scenes, one between Stockwell and Richardson, the other between Stockwell and Robards. For perhaps the only time in their lives, they speak the naked, scalding truth of what they feel about each other. As the scenes progress and the truth becomes more and more agonizing, the lenses get wider and wider, the camera gets lower and lower, the light harsher but darker, as the whole story of these people gets wrapped in night and the final, terrible truths are articulated.

All in all, it was as complex a lens, light, and camera position plan as any I've ever done, and in my view, it contributes enormously to a unique interpretation of the material.

The Verdict, Andrzej Bartkowiak, photographer. The movie was about a man's salvation, his fight to rid himself of his past.

I wanted as "old" a look as possible. Art direction had a lot to contribute, and we'll deal with that later. But light mattered enormously.

One day I brought a beautiful edition of Caravaggio's paintings to my meeting with Andrzej. I said, "Andrzej, *there's* the feeling I'm after. There's something ancient here, something from a long time ago. What is it?" Andrzej studied the pictures. Then, with his charming Polish accent, he pinpointed it. "It's chiaroscuro," he said. "A very strong light source, almost always from the side, not above. And on the other side, no soft fill light, only shadows. Once in a while he'll use the reflective light of a metal source on the dark side." He pointed to a young boy holding a golden salver. On the shadow side of the boy's face, one could discern a slight golden hue. And that's what Andrzej carried out in the lighting of the movie.

Daniel, Andrzej Bartkowiak, photographer. Once again we start with the theme: Who pays for the passions and commitments of the parents? The children. In addition, there is the complex time problem (jumping forward and backward in time).

Daniel is the story of a young man coming back to life. Loosely based on the lives and deaths of Julius and Ethel Rosenberg, it tells of Daniel's search for some meaning in his parents' senseless deaths. The parents belong to that group of thirties leftists who felt young forever, whose lives were filled with idealism and hope, until it all collapsed, personally and politically. In addition, his sister has a nervous breakdown and, unable to recover from the horrors of her childhood, sinks slowly into death. I used to think of it as the story of a young man digging himself out of his own grave.

I must pause a moment for another technical discussion. The sun's rays and the chemical composition of movie film are not a happy marriage. Untreated, any day scene shot outdoors, in cloud or in sunshine, will come out an almost mono-chromatic blue. To compensate for this, we put an amber-colored filter in the camera. This corrects the light so that the film emerges with normal colors intact. This filter is called an "85." When we shoot on an interior location with windows that let daylight in, we put enormous sheets of 85s over the windows to accomplish the same thing.

For *Daniel,* Andrzej suggested that we shoot all the scenes of the grown-up children *without* the 85. It gave everything a ghostly, cold, blue pallor, including flesh tones. For consist-ency in interior scenes, we added blue gelatins to the lights.

The parents, on the other hand, trapped in an idealized past, were treated in the amber glow of the 85s. It was *added* to their scenes, *interior* and exterior. At the beginning of the picture, we used *double* 85s on them. As Daniel slowly comes back to life, we started adding 85s to his scenes and removing them from the scenes of the past with his parents. With the parents, we went from double 85s to single 85s to half 85s to quarter 85s. On Daniel's scenes we added quarter 85s, then half 85s, then full 85s. Finally, in a scene toward the end of the picture, when both children visit the parents in jail, we were back to normal color. Daniel had purged himself of his obsessive pain, and life could now resume for him.

Every picture I've made has had this kind of attention paid to the camera. The work with the cameraman is as close as with the writer and the actors. As much as anyone, the photographer can harm or gloriously fulfill my purpose in doing the picture in the first place. During shooting, most directors' closest relationship is with the cameraman. That's why most directors work with the same cameraman year after year, as long as the style can be achieved.

The overriding consideration for me, as is apparent in all these examples, is that the techniques come from the material. They should change as the material changes. Sometimes it's important not to do anything with the camera, to just shoot it "straight." And equally important for me is that all this work stay hidden. Good camera work is not pretty pictures. It should augment and reveal the theme as fully as the actors and directors do. The light Sven Nykvist has created for so many of Ingmar Bergman's movies is directly connected to what those movies are about. The light in *Winter Light* is totally different than the light in *Fanny and Alexander*. The difference in lighting is related to the difference in the themes of the movies. That's the true beauty in movie photography.

6

ART DIRECTION AND CLOTHES
Does Faye Dunaway Really Have
the Skirt Taken in in Sixteen Different Places?

The answer is yes. She does. And she's right. Nothing can make actors feel more comfortable or uncomfortable than the clothes their characters are wearing. Aside from comfort, however, clothes contribute an enormous amount to the style of the picture.

When Betty Bacall makes her first appearance in *Murder on the Orient Express,* she's wearing a full-length peach-colored bias-cut velvet dress with a matching hat and egret feather. Jacqueline Bisset, for her first appearance, wears a full-length blue silk dress, a matching jacket with a white ermine collar, and a tiny pillbox hat with a feather. Now, Tony Walton (who did the clothes) knows that nobody gets on a train dressed like that. But what people actually wear isn't the point. In fact, what people really wear when getting on a train is the last thing we would have considered. The object was to thrust the audience into a world it never knew—to create a feeling of how glamorous things used to be. The opening titles were geared to this. I personally shot the satin that was to be the background for the titles. Tony chose the typeface.

I said earlier that there are no unimportant decisions in a movie. Along with camera, art direction (the settings) and costume design are the most important elements in creating the style—in other words, the look—of the movie. In today's films, the title is production designer. That title came into being when William Cameron Menzies served as production designer on *Gone With the Wind*. He was in charge of every visual aspect of the movie: not just clothes and sets but camera, special effects (the burning of Atlanta), and, eventually, the laboratory work on the release prints. Today, production designer is a fancier title for art director.

Tony Walton was both art director and costume designer for *Murder on the Orient Express*. We've done seven pictures together. He's not only superb at his job, but he also makes an artistic contribution over and above his own departments. I respect his opinion on script, casting, editing, camera work, every part of moviemaking. He's the personification of what I mean when I talk about working with the best. He makes *me* work harder and better.

We had an interesting problem on *Orient Express*. Earlier, I talked about backlight as a component of glamorous photography. But you need space for backlight, and train compartments are small. Tony had gone over to Belgium to see the Wagon-Lits storage sheds, where the old railway cars were kept. He reported back that the real thing was more glamorous than anything he could design. So he disassembled the interior paneling in Belgium, stripping the wood from the steel cars they were mounted on, and shipped it over to England. There the panels were laid out on the floor and reassembled on plywood flats, so we could move the walls in and out for camera positions or lights. Once a compartment was assembled, Tony began polishing the wood. The painters polished and polished. What Tony and Geoff Unsworth, the cameraman, had decided was to hit the highly polished surface with light and let its reflection serve as backlight. It wasn't as powerful as direct light, but it served the purpose.

Richness was the order of the day. Lalique glass panels, real silver on the tables, velvet on compartment seats. When we couldn't find a restaurant ornate enough for the picture, Tony converted the mezzanine of an old movie palace in London into a restaurant.

No detail was spared in creating a glamorous look. Would white or green crème de menthe look more beautiful served on a silver salver? We decided on green. For the Princess Dragomiroff, two French poodles or two Pekingese? The Pekes. For a vegetable cart in the Istanbul station, cabbages or oranges? Oranges because they'd look better when they spilled onto the dark-gray floor. And so on and so on. Tony, Geoff, and I discussed and discussed, and then we decided. Polishing every tile.

Tony and I took a very different approach on *Prince of the City*. I said earlier that the light would progress from brighter on the background, to a balance between background and foreground, to the last third of the movie where only the foreground would be lit. Art direction had its own arc or progression, too. Early in the movie, we tried to make every background as "busy" as possible. Out on the street, lots of automobiles, people, neon signs (*cuchos fritos* were a favorite). If the scene took place in an office, the walls were crowded with bulletin boards and diplomas, federal and local flags hung on stands. We filled the courtrooms with people and gave them no instructions on what to wear. But as the picture progressed, we tightened the visual reins. There were spectators in the courtrooms, but all wearing dark blue or black clothes, there were fewer decorations on walls, emptier streets. And for the final third of the picture, the sets, like the leading character, were stripped bare: nothing on the walls, no one in the streets, and, for a climactic courtroom scene, no spectators, just the bare wooden benches. This helped subtly to reinforce Ciello's increasing isolation, the loss of human contact, as he betrayed one partner after another.

In the last scene of the picture, Danny Ciello is addressing a graduating class at the Police Academy. The location picked was an amphitheater classroom. Because of the raised tiers of seats, faces stood out. Some people wore blue policemen's shirts, others wore sport jackets, and there were dresses among the female cops. Danny Ciello was back facing the consequences of his actions: a confrontation between himself and a new class of police personnel, the very people he had destroyed.

Prince of the City had over 125 locations, both interior and exterior. Their selection was critical in the visual design of the movie.

Many years earlier, I'd gone to Rome to learn from Carlo Di Palma, the great Italian cameraman. I needed help in the use of color. Carlo taught me a vital lesson. When we were picking locations in Rome, he said that the secret lay in picking the right place to begin with and then doing as *little* as possible with it. Given a choice between two equally good exteriors or interiors, pick the one that is already the right color, the one that takes the least alteration by the use of light. Paint if you have to, but try to find places that are closest to what you want to end up with. Elementary as it sounds, it opened a whole new approach for me, and this later guided me in *Prince of the City.*

Carlo admitted that finding perfect locations wasn't always possible. Sometimes the season is wrong or permission isn't granted. Logistics may make a place unusable or it's not available when the schedule demands. He told me rather shamefacedly that he had once painted the grass greener for a picture he did with Antonioni. But, he said, that was the exception.

A natural result of the careful location selection is that we often evolve a color palette for a movie. *The Verdict* is about a man haunted by his past. Ed Pisoni, a former assistant of Tony's, was the art director. I told him we'd use only autumnal colors, colors with a feeling of age. That immediately eliminated blue, pink, light green, and light yellow. We looked for browns, russets, deep yellows, burnt orange, burgundy reds, autumnal hues. Studio sets were done in those colors. If we got stuck on a location and had an unwanted color, we got permission to repaint it.

Phil Rosenberg is a wonderful art director with whom I've worked many times. On *Garbo Talks,* a light, fluffy piece, Phil and I decided that the palette would be Necco Wafers. Charm was an important part of the movie. For those of you too young to remember, Necco Wafers were a wonderful kids' candy roll. Inside the package were perhaps twenty-five sugar wafers in various pastel colors: very light green, pink, tan, aqua, white. They reminded me of a Mediterranean seaside village, one pastel piled on top of another.

In *Daniel,* the palette was critical. Every color that was used for the parents had to be compatable with the heavy use of 85s that gave the parents' scenes the golden, warm amber glow we were after. The scenes with the grown-up children had to allow an emphasis on the blue or cold side. A warm brown would have fought against what we wanted to achieve with the grown children, and blue would have hurt us in the scenes with the parents.

In *The Morning After,* we looked for expanses of high color. No color was excluded, but we wanted one color to dominate each scene. Jane Fonda's rooms were various shades of pink. In the chapter on camera work, I discussed what we did with filters to enhance the color of the sky. When I saw the orange sky in rushes, it was so shocking that I thought the audience might need some preparation. The previous scene—which fortunately I hadn't yet shot—was set at an outdoor fast-food joint. I ordered orange umbrellas over the tables so the ambient light for the scene itself would take on an orange hue. For the title sequence, I found a series of walls, yellow, red, brown, blue, and just had Fonda walking dejectedly past them. Buildings were deep blue, baby pink, any strong color. Los Angeles can provide an endless supply of that kind of decor.

On other pictures, I've wanted a hodgepodge. For *Q & A* and *Dog Day Afternoon,* everything had to feel accidental—no planning, no color control. On both pictures, I told the art director and the costume designer *not* to consult with each other. I wanted no relationship between the sets and the costumes. Whatever happened happened.

Sometimes, rather than selecting a color palette, I've picked an architectural style. In *The Verdict,* we used both a very narrow color selection and older architecture. No modern buildings were seen in the movie. Conversely, in *Guilty as Sin,* I wanted nothing but the most modern buildings we could find. Fortunately, we were shooting the picture in Toronto, with its superb modern architecture. In no time at all, Phil Rosenberg had found enough locations for us to be able to pick and choose.

By now, most cameramen are so skillful that it's hard to tell whether a scene has been shot in the studio or on location. I base my decision on two factors. One is cost. As a general rule, if I'm going to take more than two days to shoot the scene, I'll build it in the studio. That's usually more economical, since we carry an enormous number of extra people and equipment on location. Of course, if the set is ornate or has very expensive detail, it may be cheaper to shoot the scene on location even if it runs more than two days. A second factor is whether or not I need "wild walls"—walls that are movable and removable. Sometimes the scene requires complex camera moves or, because of long lenses, distance from the set itself. In that case you have to go into the studio.

Dog Day Afternoon presented a difficult problem. Because so much of the action took place inside the bank, it would've been simpler to build the bank in the studio. But I felt it would be better for the staging and the camera if I could move freely between the street and the bank. We came up with the perfect solution. We found an excellent street that had a lower warehouse floor we could rent. We built the bank inside the warehouse so I could have my "wild walls" and still have constant access between the street and the interior of the bank.

Not only location versus studio, but location versus location can enormously affect the cost of the picture. I always try to keep my locations as close together as possible. The reason is simple. If I finish a location, exterior or interior, at eleven in the morning, moving to a second location within an hour or two can save a lot of money. We can at least start lighting and might even get some shooting done.

On *Prince of the City,* we found an extraordinary building, the old U.S. Customs House in lower Manhattan. It has five stories and an interior courtyard, and it occupies a full square city block. It was empty at the time, no longer in use. The building's architecture was amazing. On the ground floor, eighteen-foot ceilings, wainscoting, carved ceilings and mantel, windows nine feet tall, paneling, tiled floors. Ascending, each story got smaller and simpler—lower ceilings, less ornate—until the top-floor rooms were no more than a series of boxes. We were able to use the one building for almost every office scene in the movie. And we needed a lot of offices, bouncing up and back between Washington and New York, federal offices, city offices, and state D.A.'s offices, police offices for every rank. Each office had a different view outside its window because we were in a four-sided building. In addition, the inner courtyard gave offices in the interior of the building a whole new set of views out the windows. Finding twelve offices in the same building probably saved us four shooting days. And that's a *lot* of money.

Sometimes a scenic concept gets lost in execution. The idea I had for *The Wiz* was that reality could be turned into an urban fantasy. We would use real locations but treat them in such a way that the locations would become truly fantastical. But I came to grief on the first location scouting trip. I wanted the Cowardly Lion to be discovered at—where else?—the New York Public Library, Forty-second Street and Fifth Avenue. Tony Walton, Albert Whitlock, and I stood across the street, gazing at the building, for four hours. Whitlock is one of the foremost matte-painting and special-effects cameramen in the business. He was a master at combining painted glass backgrounds with live foreground action. "Albert, when a door opens, can we see sky behind it rather than the interior of the building?" I would ask. The answer was no. Every idea I had to fantasize that building was, Albert told me, impossible. Slowly my heart sank. We finally decided to build the set in the studio.

Then more and more studio work was added to what had originally been a heavy location picture. Fantasy took over to such
a degree that the urban quality was lost. In the most expensive
sequence, to be shot at the World Trade Center, we never
figured how brutal the wind could be when it was channeled
between those two towers. They formed a natural wind tun-
nel. The hats of the male and female models were very important in establishing "attitude." And the hats wouldn't stay on
because of the wind. Pins didn't work. Bands around the back
of the head didn't work. Finally, the bands were placed under
the chin. The hats stayed on, but the look was ruined. From
large things to small, I felt the concept going out the window.
It was my own fault. I simply didn't know enough technically
to master all departments, particularly special effects. Even
though I had very good people in charge, there were just
too many departments that were going their own way. I could
feel the visual approach leaking out of my hands like water
through my fingers. It happens.

To talk about art direction in black-and-white movies is to
talk about something extinct. But it was exciting while it
lasted. Dick Sylbert's work on *The Pawnbroker* was superb. This
was a picture about creating our own prisons. Starting with
the pawnshop itself, Dick created a series of cages: wire mesh,
bars, locks, alarms, anything that would reinforce a sense of
entrapment. The locations were picked with this in mind. The
supposedly wide-open spaces of suburbia at the beginning of
the picture were cut up by fences clearly delineating each
house's 125-foot frontage. For the critical scene where Rod
Steiger tells Geraldine Fitzgerald of his guilt at being alive, we
found an apartment on the West Side of Manhattan that overlooked the New York Central railroad yards. Throughout the

scene you can see and hear freight cars being shunted from track to track. That kind of visual and auditory corroboration of a scene's context is invaluable.

In *The Fugitive Kind,* also designed by Sylbert, the main action took place in a dry-goods store. We discussed trying to place Brando against light, uncluttered backgrounds. Dick designed the store so that its second story was cream-colored. By lowering the camera, we almost always framed Brando against a lighter background.

These elements may sound small, but they add up. They're a necessary part of the unity each production demands. Color is highly subjective. Blue or red may mean totally different things to you and me. But as long as my interpretation of a color is consistent, eventually you'll become aware (subconsciously, I hope) of how I'm using that color and what I'm using it for.

A great deal of art direction and costume design affects performance. When Kate Hepburn walked onto the set of the living room of *Long Day's Journey Into Night,* she smiled and said, "It's bone-chillingly marvelous. Which is my chair? Each person always develops a fondness for her own chair." She was right. I said, "The rocker's yours." We had anticipated such a question. Already in place beside her rocker were the women's magazines of the period and the knitting that her character barely touched. I had a wonderful propman, who always had the mail in a house addressed to the character. Papers on a desk were specific to that person and his profession. When the actor opened a folder in a conference room scene, papers in the folder were about the subject to be discussed. These things help the actor's concentration immeasurably. They put him into a real world, a world that exists on more than just the written page of the script. On *A Stranger Among Us,* the Judaica in the rabbi's house was so rich that we had a security man on set when we weren't using it.

Nothing helps actors more than the clothes they wear. Ann Roth is an amazing costume designer. She can take the most everyday clothes and turn them into some sort of contribution, to both the actor and the picture. On *Family Business,* Sean Connery came into rehearsal after having been with Ann for a clothes fitting. He looked happy. I asked him how it had gone. "She's bloody marvelous," he said. "She's given me the whole bloody character now." That's the greatest compliment an actor can give. It's the equivalent of saying, "We're all making the same picture."

SHOOTING THE MOVIE
At Last!

Sets, clothes, camera concept, script, casting, rehearsals, schedule, financing, cash flow, insurance examinations, locations, cover sets (interiors that we shoot if the weather is wrong for exterior shooting), hair, makeup, tests, composer, editor, sound editor have all been decided. Now we're shooting the movie, at last.

My alarm will go off at seven. I'll get picked up at eight, so I have an hour for coffee, a bagel, *The New York Times,* and getting my head ready for the day's work. By now, my body is so disciplined that I wake up about five minutes before the alarm goes off. I put on my robe and tiptoe out of the room. I've laid out my blue jeans, shirt, socks, sneakers in another room so that I don't disturb my wife. With my coffee, I scan page 1. The object is to get as quickly as possible to the crossword puzzle, so that I can empty my mind completely and start the day fresh. A second cup of coffee, and I'm ready to open my script and look over the scene or scenes scheduled for today.

Facing this page is the call sheet. It's for a picture called *A Stranger Among Us* (originally titled *Close to Eden*). The story is about a detective who goes undercover into the Hasidic community to find a murderer. Melanie Griffith played the detective. The murder involved the diamond center, a block-long area in New York where many Hasidim work. Though I'm using this picture as an example, the procedure described in the following pages holds true for most of the pictures I've done.

The call sheet is our bible. It's what we're going to shoot that day. If it's not on the call sheet, we don't need it. I've numbered the sections here for easy reference.

Section 1 is self-evident, except for "Shoot Day #22." That means it's our twenty-second day of shooting. The crew call right below it says that the crew will be ready to start work at 8:30 a.m. The shooting call of 9:00 a.m. means that Andrzej has about a half hour of lighting to do before we'd be ready for the actors.

Section 2: The Set Description starts with "Interior—Diamond Center—D." "D" stands for "Day." (If it were a night scene, it would say "N.") It's followed by a brief description of the content of the scene. Next to it is the scene number. On the big scheduling board made up before the picture began, each scene was numbered, according to the numbers assigned on the final shooting script. The numbers are consecutive. (A long scene may contain several numbers.) Next are the character numbers, also from the scheduling board, a quick reference to the characters who would be working on particular days. (The numbers reappear in section 3.) Next comes page count. Shooting scripts are broken down into eighths of a page. Generally, you try to shoot three pages a day. Forty days is the

```
TITLE CLOSE TO EDEN                                  DATE: TUES. 10/22/91
DIRECTOR SIDNEY LUMET          CALL SHEET         SHOOT DAY#: #22
ASST DIR HARRIS/PENOTTI/SMITH (718) 555-1234        CREW CALL: 8:30A
                                                 SHOOTING CALL: 9A
[1]
```

SET DESCRIPTION	SCENES	CHARACTER	PAGES	LOCATION
: IF NOT DONE:				: KAUFMAN ASTORIA
: INT-DIAMOND CTR-D	64	1,2,4,5,9	4/8	: STUDIOS
: ''EMILY LISTEN'S TO				: 34-12 36th St.
C.D.''				
:				: Astoria, NY
: THEN:				: ''STAGE E''
: INT-DIAMOND CTR-D	58	1,2,4,5,9,15,16	3-1/8	:
: ''BROS. TALK				:
SECURITY''				
: BEGIN:				:
: INT-DIAMOND CTR-D	86,88	1,2,4,5,9,15,16	4-3/8	:
: ''C.D./BUST BROS.''				:
:				:
: **DAILIES @ 5:30P.M.**				:
:				:
:				:
:				:
[2]				

CAST		CHARACTER	P/U	M/U	SET
: 1	: Melanie Griffith	: Emily	: P/U @ 7A	: 7:30A	: 9A
: 2	: Eric Thal	: Ariel	: P/U @ 6:30A	: 7A	: 9A
: 4	: Mia Sara	: Leah	: P/U @ 7:30A	: 8A	: 9A
: 5	: Tracy Pollan	: Mara	: P/U @ 7:30A	: 8A	: 9A
: 9	: Ro'ee Levi	: Mendel	: RPT @ 7:30A	: 7:30A	: 9A
:15	: James Gandolfini	: Tony Baldessari	: RPT @ 7:15A	: 7:15A	: 9A
:16	: Chris Collins	: C.Baldessari	: RPT @ 7:15A	: 7:15A	: 9A
[3]					

STANDINS AND EXTRAS	PROPS AND SPECIAL INSTRUCTIONS
: STANDINS # 1,2,4,5 RPT @ 8:15A	: MONEY, PATEK WATCH, DISCMAN,
	JACKET
:	: OF JEWELS, RECEIPT BOOK, EMILY'S
: 55 B.G. RPT @ 7:30A	: BADGE, EMILY'S GUN, TRANSMITTER,
: TO INCLUDE:	: ENVELOPE OF MONEY.
: 25-''CORE SERVERS'' W/2	:
CHANGES(RECALLED)	
: 30-CUSTOMERS W/2 CHANGES	:
:	:
:	:
:	:
: [4]	:

CREW CALL: 8:30A

DIRECTOR: P/U @ 8A	SOUND: 8:30A	SCENIC: 8:30A
ASST DIR: 7A/8:30A	GRIPS: 8:30A	MAKEUP: 7A
SCRIPT: 8:30A	PROPS: 8:30A	HAIR: 7A
CAMERA: 8:30A	ELECT: 8:30A	WARDROBE: 7A
STILLS: 9A	CARPS: PER D.RESEIGNE	COFFEE &: RDY @ 7A
P.A.S : PER J.PENOTTI	DRESSER: PER D.RESEIGNE	LUNCH: —
STUNTS: O/C	SPEC EFX: O/C	VIDEO: —

[5]

ADVANCE SCHEDULE		TRANSPORTATION
: WEDNESDAY 10/23/91		: PER T.REILLY/J.NUGENT
: COMPLETE:		: P/U S.LUMET @ 8A
: INT-DIAMOND CTR-D	SC.86,88	: P/U M.GRIFFITH @ 7A
: THEN:		: P/U E.THAL @ 6:30A
: EXT-LEVINE'S CAR	SC.82	: P/U M.SARA @ 7:30A
: EXT-EMILY'S CAR(RESHOOT)	SC.106	: P/U T.POLLAN @ 7:30A
:		:
: THURSDAY 10/24/91		: ------------------------------
: (LATER CALL TO ALLOW FOR RIGGING)		: CONTINUE ADVANCE SCHEDULE:
: INT-DIAMOND CTR-D	SC.90,92	: FRIDAY 10/25/91
: IF NOT COMPLETE:	SC.82,106	: INT-LEAH'S ROOM-D
: INT-LEAH'S ROOM-D	SC.38,34A	
:		

: [6]

usual time for a 120-page script of a simple movie. Movies with heavy special effects, battle scenes, big stunts, and crowds usually run much longer. "Location" is clear: the set is in the studio.

Section 3 starts with the character number, the actor's name, and the character name. "P/U" stands for "pickup." It's the time their teamster driver is to pick them up at home. Under that, "RPT" stands for "reporting time." These actors are not being picked up and must find their way to the studio on their own. "M/U" stands for "makeup," the time the actor is to be in the makeup room. "Set" means that they are due on set at 9:00 a.m., dressed, made up, and ready to go.

Section 4 starts with the stand-ins. They substitute for the actors while lighting is being done. Below them, "55 B.G. RPT 7:30A" means fifty-five background (the polite word for extras) report at 7:30 a.m. After they are checked in by the assistant director, their clothes are OK'd by costume; after a stop for coffee, they must be in place for lighting by 8:30. Those who supply their own clothes get an allowance for them. The set is a jewelry exchange store with many counters. That's why the fifty-five extras are broken down into "25 core servers." These extras will play the salespeople behind the counters, and thirty customers. "W/2 changes" indicates a change of clothing they are to have brought. Going back to the scene numbers, you'll see three different entries. The scenes take place on different days; thus the change of clothes. "(Recalled)" means that these people should be the same ones who worked the day before. If all goes as planned and we get more than one scene, the customers will also change clothes. The foreground customers from Scene 64 will be placed in the background for Scene 58. "Props and Special Instructions" lists all the props that are needed for specific action in the scene. This is over and above the set dressing.

Section 5 lists the pickup time or reporting time for everybody other than actors: the crew. "Stills" refers to the still photographer, who shoots all those thrilling shots you see on posters in movie lobbies. "P.A." stands for production assistants. PAs are the gofers of movies, hardworking, underpaid film students or relatives of the producer who want to learn about movies. Good PAs are a godsend and can work their way into the union after several pictures. "Grips" are stagehands. "Carps" and "Dressers" are the carpenters and set dressers who are working on upcoming sets being built on the same stage. "Per D. Reseigne" tells them to report for orders from the construction chief, Dick Reseigne. "Stunts: O/C" and "Spec Efx: O/C" means that there's no stunt work or special effects that day. Notice that "Coffee &" is ready first.

Section 6 is again self-evident. Repeating the pickup times

under "Transportation" is for the sake of the teamster drivers, who get confused if they have to read too much.

I'm out my door five minutes early. I'm always early. The station wagon is waiting for me. Burtt Harris, the assistant director, is stretched out on the backseat, a container of coffee in hand, his eyes closed. Two blocks away, I can see Andrzej pedaling toward us furiously. He lives on a boat on the Hudson River and bikes to my house every morning. I worry constantly, especially in bad weather. I once had to replace a cameraman during shooting. It's a nightmare. A hug for Andrzej, a grunt to Burtt. I get into the front seat. Andrzej throws his bike in the back, and we're off.

I like to ride to work with the AD and the cameraman. One of us may have thought of something that had been omitted. Or a new problem may have come up. Maybe Melanie called Burtt last night to say she felt a cold coming on. Can we shoot around her till her voice loosens up? Or Andrzej may report that they ran into a problem when they were roughing in the lighting last night. He's going to need another half hour. (I hate that. I like to put the actors to work as close to their "On Set" time as possible.) These sorts of problems always arise. They're not too serious.

The ride to the studio is uneventful and quiet. Andrzej reads the newspaper, Burtt dozes, I study my script and think. The driver knows I don't like conversation or the radio. What we're doing matters. It needs concentration. Last night I thought of a camera move during Eric's speech. That means when I turn around to shoot Melanie's side, I'll need a different wall put back up. I tell Burtt. He mumbles, "Gotcha," and I know it will be done.

We pull up at the studio. A PA is waiting out front. He says, "Sidney's here," into his walkie-talkie. We do that with all the essential personnel. We don't want to wait until ten minutes have gone by to find out that somebody's late.

Andrzej heads for the coffee, Burtt to the soundstage, and I walk to the makeup rooms to say good morning to the actors. Generally we just have a quick hug in the makeup room. I may say that rushes looked good, but I don't necessarily talk about rushes. I don't want the actors to expect automatic praise. They have to trust me, and squandering praise destroys its meaning.

By 8:25, I'm on the set. I don't know about other directors, but I rarely leave the set when lighting is being done. First of all, there's no place I'd rather be. Second, I love to watch how the cameraman is attacking the problem. Each one works differently. My presence is also good for the crew. They work harder. Is the camera operator rehearsing with the dolly grip? He should be. Has the focus puller gotten his marks (the distances between the lens and the actors)? Sometimes, when working with a wide-open stop, he has to mark the distances with chalk on the floor. How good is the grip with cutters and nets? A cutter is an opaque board or slat that cuts light off from any place the cameraman doesn't want it to hit. A net reduces the amount of light. Each cutter or net is held in place by a grip stand, a three-legged stand with bars that can be angled in any direction to hold the cutter in place. Each grip stand requires a sandbag so that the stand doesn't fall if someone trips over it. And *everybody* trips over it. The sheer detail of lighting a set is mind-boggling. That's why it takes so long.

The stand-ins are wearing the same colors that the actors will wear in the scene. If the stand-in wears a dark jacket and the actor shows up in a white shirt, it will necessitate some relighting. That means time. And time is lot of money.

In the meantime, Burtt and the second AD are blocking in

the extras. "You stand here." "You cross here." They work as quietly as they can, because Andrzej is constantly instructing the electricians and grips on lighting. Andrzej will turn to the third AD and say, "Fifteen minutes." The third AD will rush off to tell the actors that we'll be ready for them in fifteen minutes.

The work of blocking the extras can be critical. Often the entire reality of the scene can be ruined by staging them badly. You've seen it a hundred times. The star comes out of the courtroom! Microphones are shoved in his face! Cameras are clicking! And in the chaos? Somehow there are no people between the star and the movie camera. Or someone's in front, but he's very short. Ugh!

Nowhere was the crowd more critical than in *Dog Day Afternoon.* We had a minimum of five hundred people a day for over three weeks. Before we started, Burtt and I broke them down to individual characters: Sixteen yentas (busybodies), who were then broken down even further—"You two know each other, you four hate those two because they're too good at mah-jongg." These six teenagers were playing hooky. These four arrive later and stay for the show rather than go to the movies. We made an enormous diagram of the whole area, placing each extra as he arrived on the scene. A group of four truck-drivers was put on a particular corner. Later that night, when a group of sixteen gays from the Village arrived to demonstrate in support of Pacino's character, the truckdrivers were in the right position to start a fight. The skill with which the extras were directed in *Schindler's List* is vital to the brilliance of that movie. There are no small decisions in moviemaking.

When we actually started shooting *Dog Day Afternoon,* I talked to the extras for over an hour from atop a ladder. The individuals they were playing were explained to them in detail.

Since we knew we'd never be able to keep the people who actually lived in the neighborhood out of the shots, we got the extras to involve the neighborhood people in the situations. It got so participatory that by the second week of shooting we didn't have to tell anybody how to react. They just did what came naturally, and it was wonderful.

One of the reasons I prefer working in New York is that real actors work as extras. They are members of the Screen Actors Guild, and many appear regularly on and off Broadway. Many have worked their way into speaking parts. In Los Angeles, extras belong to the Screen Extras Guild, a special union for people who do nothing but extra work. Often they don't even know what picture they are working on. They come from all over the country, shaving their heads, dressing like Minnie Pearl or Minnie Mouse—emphasizing whatever physical characteristic they feel might get them hired, just wanting a job for 180 days a year. If they can get into a shot of less than five people, they become "special business" and receive a slight increase in their day's pay. If they have evening clothes, it'll be stated on their résumé and they'll get paid extra for a dinner jacket or an evening gown. They are then called "dress extras." It's thoroughly depressing.

You can tell that shooting time is close now, because the star's makeup and hair people arrive on the set, slowly, languorously, carrying their makeup boxes, Kleenex, brushes, combs. If I sound a bit peevish, it's because quite often these people aren't really "making the same movie" as the rest of us. Their first obligation is to the star's looks. They fuss, they coddle, they make themselves seemingly indispensable. And some stars are suckers for it. After all, if the star does three pictures in a year, the makeup person is going to work close to thirty-six weeks. And their salaries, because they are part of the star's perks, are outrageous: $4,000 a week for thirty-six weeks? Not bad. And that still leaves them sixteen weeks off to go to Acapulco.

The arrival of makeup and hair is the cue for the sound department to wire the actors, if necessary. On a large set, the microphone on the boom may not reach all the actors. A tiny microphone is then placed somewhere on the chest. It has a wire that runs to a hidden transmitter: somewhere on the actor. A woman wearing tight clothes may have it strapped to her inner thigh. On the take, the transmitter is turned on and sends a radio signal that allows the soundman to record the dialogue in his receiver. Occasionally a take is ruined because two chatty Pakistani cabdrivers are driving past the studio and we pick up the wrong transmitter.

Andrzej is ready. The actors are on set. The AD calls for "Bells!" A sharp bell that would frighten a fireman sounds three times on the stage and just outside. We take our first rehearsal. "Don't work," I tell the actors. "Just make the moves and use the volume you'll be using, for sound."

I don't want the actors wasting any emotion. They are in for a long day, and I want them to save their emotions for the take. After the first rehearsal we always have things to fix. Up until now, all lighting was done on the "second team" (the stand-ins). Now, with the "first team" (the actors themselves), there are corrections to be made. This is normal, and none of the actors mind. Then, because the actor moves at a different pace than the stand-in, a camera movement will have to be adjusted. The varying physical characteristics of the actors may also necessitate changes. Sean Connery is six feet four. Dustin Hoffman isn't. Trying to get them in a tight two-shot presents some problems. I tend to shoot everything at eye level, but I'm talking about *my* eye level. And I'm Dustin's height (five feet six). For example: "Sean, give me a Groucho." That means: Will you start lowering your body *before* you sit. As Sean comes toward us, the camera has to pan up to hold his head in the frame. Because of his height, this can mean that the camera is seeing over the top of the set, shooting into the lights. We don't want to move the lights after all that work. And unless we want a ceiling for dramatic reasons, we don't want to put one in. Sean does the Groucho. Most experienced actors can do it without breaking their concentration. "Give me a slight banana on that cross from left to right." That means: As you're crossing, arc slightly away from the camera for the same reason that you gave us the Groucho. Otherwise we'd be shooting off set. The script girl may whisper in my ear, "He's picking up the drink a little late." When we shot over his shoulder yesterday, he picked up his drink at the beginning of the sentence. If he's now picking it up at the end of the sentence, I'll have a problem later in the editing room when I want to cut from yesterday's shot to today's.

These technical considerations are mere refinements rather than problems. Most actors are used to them after a few pictures. Henry Fonda was more accurate than the script girl. On *12 Angry Men,* the wonderful Faith Hubley was script girl and had noted that the cigarette was lit on such and such a line. Fonda said it was on the preceding line. We shot it both ways. Henry was right.

Andrzej has fine-tuned his lighting. We've done our Grouchos and bananas. If the shot has a complicated camera move, I'll rehearse it as many times as necessary, until the camera operator, dolly grip, and focus puller are comfortable. A good dolly grip is indispensable. It's not only a question of getting the camera to the right position—"hitting the mark." He also has to be able to watch and "feel" the actor. Often, during a take, the actor's tempo will change drastically. He may go much faster or slower than he did in rehearsal. The camera obviously has to keep pace with him. And that's the dolly grip's responsibility.

During these rehearsals, I'm constantly telling the actors not to work full out, just to walk it until all mechanical problems are out of the way. Because of our rehearsals back at the Ukrainian Home, the actors are well prepared. Very often we'll hit it on the first take. Many movie crews approach the first take as a dress rehearsal. I knock that idea out of their heads on day one. On the first shot, I'll pick something that involves no acting and is mechanically simple: Dustin Hoffman walks down the street and goes into the building. I call, "Cut!" and ask the camera operator, "Good for you?" He says, "Yes." I call, "Print!" and move on to the next setup. Everyone on the crew now knows that Take 1 can wind up on two thousand screens this Christmas. This isn't a dress rehearsal. It's for real.

Technical problems are out of the way. We're ready for a take. I ask makeup to "check them out." Quickly. One of the hardest things to teach makeup and hair people is that the final thing I want the actor to be thinking about is the scene about to be played, not how he looks. Most of the time, just as you're ready to roll, they pile in with their combs, mirrors, brushes. For some actors it's just another technical consideration, but I've seen actors wave them off.

"Bells!" Now the stage is *really* silent. "Roll it." The soundman rolls his tape. When it's up to speed, he calls, "Speed." The camera operator hits the switch. The camera is up to speed. The second assistant cameraman lifts a slate in front of the camera. Printed on it are my name, Andrzej's name, the producer's name, the name of the picture, and (the only important thing) the scene number and take number. He'll call,

"Scene Sixty-eight—Take One." Then he'll slap a hinged stick onto the slate. The stick and the top of the slate have diagonal stripes on them. The stick hits the slate and makes a loud *clap*. In fact, in England, the person who does this is called the clapper boy. The diagonal stripes coming together visually and the audio *clap* provide a synchronization mark for the picture and sound track. At this point these are separate entities. The editor synchs the film this way for rushes the next day.

I'm so aware of the actor's concentration, I'll sometimes call for "end sticks" instead. I don't want that loud *clap* to disturb him at the beginning of the take. I find that slating it at the end of the take is useful for actors with little experience. The operator nods to me. I call, "Action!" Just like in the movies.

We've reached the moment of truth. My calling "Action!" says it all. Internal action. External action. Perform. Do. Acting is active, it's doing. Acting is a verb.

I pointed out earlier how little control the director has over certain vital areas. One of these is the operation of the camera. I mentioned Peter McDonald, the operator on *Murder on the Orient Express*. Peter was a kind of genius at his job, as well as being a master technically. The operator has two wheels to control the movement of the camera. One moves the camera up and down, the other moves it from side to side. A good operator can move the camera in a straight line on a perfect 45-degree angle from lower left to upper right. But Peter was far more skilled than that. He could tape a pen to the lens shade so that it stuck out in front of the camera. Then he'd put a piece of paper on a grip stand at the point of the pen. Then he'd write your name on that paper.

But it wasn't just his technical brilliance. Many operators have that. When a shot is complicated, the cameraman or I can show the operator the opening frame and the closing frame.

We can say that as the camera moves, we want to see this or that ("Pick up the wineglass on the table during the move"). But basically the operator is framing the picture at all times *during* the take. His sense of beauty or drama, his sense of rhythm, his sense of composition—all that is critical to the creativity of the shot. His technique has to be practically subconscious, because I want him watching the actor, not the corners of his frame. It's been invariably true that the best camera operators will do their best take when the actor's doing *his* best take. It sounds romantic, but it is part of the mystique of moviemaking. It was, of course, true of Peter. His eye was so creative that when he made suggestions on the composition of a shot, it was always better than what I had in mind. (Once I had an operator who, for whatever psychological reason, invariably screwed up the actor's best take. The fourth time it happened, I replaced him.)

A character shot in close-up is usually talking or reacting to one person or more. Again, to help maintain reality and concentration, I like to have the off-camera actor or actors gathered around the camera to work with the actor being photographed. Clearly, this was a must in *12 Angry Men.* Sometimes the off-camera actor doesn't really work with the on-camera actor. He may be afraid of using up the feeling if his side hasn't been shot yet. Sometimes it's a subtle form of sabotage. Visiting a set one day, I saw the star feeding off-camera lines to a day player (an actor hired for a small part on a daily basis). The star sat on a high stool and didn't even look at the other actor. In fact, her attention was riveted on her crocheting. This can create very bad feelings on a set. Whenever I see it happening, I take immediate steps by talking to the off-camera actor as gently or firmly as is needed.

This opens up an important area. When the actor is being

photographed looking at someone off-camera, he can obviously see past him to the whole darkened studio. We call this the actor's "eyeline." It can involve both sides of the camera. Just before we roll, any well-trained AD will always say, "Clear the eyeline, please." If William Holden is making love to Faye Dunaway, he doesn't want to see some teamster sipping coffee behind her. He doesn't want to see anybody other than Faye watching him, even if he has great concentration. Since most crews don't understand this, "Clear the eyeline" becomes a never-ending refrain.

Take 1 is over. I saw something I didn't like. I want to go again. The same process. "Scene Sixty-eight—Take Two." "Sticks." "Action!" Take 2 is all right, but "Let's try one more." I'll come up to the actor with a new suggestion, just to see if it will stimulate a surprise or a more spontaneous or surprising performance. Sometimes I'll say, "That's a beauty. Print it. Now, just for the hell of it, try whatever comes to mind." Sometimes the actor will ask for another take. I always go along with that. About half the time the actor does do better. Sometimes if I feel the actor is struggling with a scene, I'll call "Print" even though I don't intend to use the take. I do it as encouragement. When actors have heard "Print," they know they have a good one in the can and they relax. This frees them for something more spontaneous.

I'd like to try to explain the process I go through when I call "Print." After all is said and done, that's the reason we're doing all this. Obviously, certain shots in a movie require nothing beyond mechanical perfection. I'm not thinking of those. I'm thinking of shots that are involved with character, or critical plot points, or highly emotional moments. First, I place myself as close to the lens as possible. Sometimes I sit on the dolly, just beneath the lens. Or I tuck myself behind the operator's shoulder. This way I'm not only as close as I can get to the lens's view of the scene, but I'm also out of the actor's eyeline.

Then comes the hard part. Just before we roll, I make a quick mental check of what preceded the moment we're about to film and what comes afterward. Then I focus my concentration on what the actors are doing. From the moment the actors start working, I play the scene along with them. I say the lines inside my head, I sense their movements and feel their emotions. I'm putting myself through the scene as if I *were* them. If the camera moves, out of the corner of my eye I'm watching the lens shade to see if the move has been mechanically smooth or jerky. If at any point in the take my concentration breaks, I know that something has gone wrong. Then I'll go for another take. Sometimes, on particularly good takes, I'm so moved that I stop "doing" the scene and just watch in awe at the miracle of good acting. As I said earlier, that's life up there. When it flows like that, that's when I say "Print." Is it exhausting? You bet it is.

One of the most difficult acting scenes I've ever encountered was on *Dog Day Afternoon*. About two-thirds of the way through the movie, Pacino makes two phone calls: one to his male "wife" and lover, who's at a barbershop across the street, and the second to his "real" wife, in her home.

I knew Al would build up the fullest head of steam if we could do it in one take. The scene took place at night. The character had been in the bank for twelve hours. He had to seem spent, exhausted. When we're that tired, emotions flow more easily. And that's what I wanted.

There was an immediate problem. The camera holds only a thousand feet of film. That's a bit over eleven minutes. The two phone calls ran almost fifteen minutes. I solved it by putting two cameras next to each other, the lenses as close together as was physically possible. Naturally, both lenses were the same—55 mm, as I remember. When camera 1 had used about 850 feet, we would roll camera 2 while camera 1 was still running. I knew that there would be an intercut of the wife somewhere in the final film, which would allow me to cut to the film in camera 2. But Al would have acted out the two phone calls continuously, just as it happened in real life.

I wanted Al's concentration at its peak. I cleared the set and then, about five feet behind the camera, put up black flats so that even the rest of the physical set was blocked out. The propman had rigged the phones so the off-camera actors could speak into phones across the street and Al would really hear them on his phone.

One more thing occurred to me. One of the best ways of accumulating emotion is to go as rapidly as possible from one take to the next. The actor begins the second take on the emotional level he reached at the end of the first take. Sometimes I don't even cut the camera. I'll say quietly, "Don't cut the camera—everybody back to their opening positions and we're going again. OK from the top: Action!" By the way, I always call "Action" in the mood of the scene. If it's a gentle moment, I'll say "Action" just loud enough for the actors to hear me. If it's a scene that requires a lot of energy, I'll bark out "Action" like a drill seargent. It's like a conductor giving the upbeat.

I knew a second take would mean a serious interruption for Al. We'd have to reload one of the cameras. Reloading a magazine of film can be quite disruptive. The magazines are usually kept in the darkroom, which is always far away. In addition, the camera cover (the Barney) we use to reduce camera noise has to be taken off; the camera has to be opened; and then the film has to be threaded through all those little gears. The whole process, done at top speed, takes two or three minutes, enough time for Al to cool off. So I put up a black tent to block off both cameras and the men operating them. We cut two holes for the lenses. And I had the second assistant cameraman (there are three men on a camera crew: operator, focus puller, and second assistant) hold an extra film magazine in his lap, in case we needed it.

We rolled. As camera 1 reached 850 feet, we rolled camera 2. The take ended. It was wonderful. But something told me to go again. Camera 2 had used only about 200 feet. I called out gently, "Al, back to the top. I want to go again." He looked at me as if I'd gone mad. He'd gone full out and was exhausted. He said, "What?! You're kidding." I said, "Al, we *have* to. Roll camera."

We rolled camera 2. It had about 800 feet left. Meanwhile, behind the camera tent, out of Al's sight, we reloaded camera 1. By the time camera 2 had used 700 feet (close to eight minutes into the take), we started the reloaded camera 1. By the end of the second take, Al didn't know where he was anymore. He finished his lines and, in sheer exhaustion, looked about helplessly. Then, by accident, he looked directly at me. Tears were rolling down my face because he'd moved me so. His eyes locked into mine and he burst into tears, then slumped over the desk he'd been sitting at. I called, "Cut! Print!" and leapt into the air. That take is some of the best film acting I've ever seen.

Peter Finch's "I'm mad as hell and I'm not going to take it anymore" speech in *Network* was done in almost the same way. In that picture it was easier, because the speech lasted only about six minutes; all I needed was to have a second camera ready. No reloading. No time lost between takes. Halfway through the speech on Take 2, Peter stopped. He was exhausted. I didn't know then of his weakened heart, but I didn't push for another take. And that's how it wound up in the finished movie: the first half of the speech from Take 2, the second half from Take 1.

Back to our day of shooting. I've started with the widest shot against wall A, as described earlier. Now I start moving in for tighter and tighter shots against the same wall. When I've finished everything that could be shot against wall A, I'll move to wall B. I try to lay out the shooting order so that we can move the basic camera position as little as possible. The smaller the move, the quicker we'll be ready, because relighting takes less time. Clearly, this isn't always possible. The actor might move around the room from wall A to wall B. Sometimes I've staged a scene so that the camera is in the center of the room and has to pan around 360 degrees. All four walls appear in the shot as the actor moves. These shots are very difficult to light. It can take four or five hours to light a shot that goes 360 degrees, sometimes a full day. Katharine Hepburn had a shot like that in *Long Day's Journey Into Night.* She circled the room twice, talking more and more frenetically as she went. Boris Kaufman took four hours to light it. I had another one in *Q & A,* as a young numbers cruncher recited polling results to a roomful of politicians. In *The Group,* we did the reverse. The girls in *The Group* would gather periodically for coffee klatches and gossip. It could be at someone's home or in a cafeteria. Each time, there would be four or five of them around a table. I wanted to link these scenes visually. The camera would dolly 360 degrees around the outside of the table, shooting *in* at the girls. We kept the camera movement quite rapid to give these scenes an airy, gay spirit, since the get-togethers were always a source of happy college memories for the characters involved.

One of the most complex lighting jobs was the first shot inside the jury room in *12 Angry Men.* The shot lasts almost eight minutes. We meet all twelve jurors. The shot starts over the fan, which will matter later in the movie, and at one point or another moves into at least a medium shot of each person. I did it on a crane. The base of the crane (the dolly) had thirteen different positions moving in and about the small set. The arm (the boom) on which the camera sat had eleven different positions left and right and eight different positions up and down. Boris Kaufman needed seven hours to light the shot. We got it on Take 4.

⌐If I'm going to make a big turnaround, going from wall A to wall C, I try to time it for the lunch hour. Generally, the construction crew (four grips, two carpenters) go to lunch an hour earlier than we do. By the time we break, anywhere between 11:30 and 1:30, they're already back and can make the changeover. They put wall C back and pull out wall A. It's more complicated than it sounds. Everything has to move—chairs, makeup tables, sound boom, camera dolly; the dressing (curtains, shelves, pictures, et cetera) comes down off wall A and has to be put back up on wall C. The paint, plaster, or wallpaper on the walls gets damaged from constant movement and has to be repaired. If ceiling pieces are being moved, the old ones have to be removed and new ones put in. The floor becomes filthy during shooting and has to be swept. Dolly tracks have to be taken up. Every lamp has to be disconnected. The main power cable has to be rerouted to the opposite side of the set.

The break is usually welcome. We've lit for perhaps an hour or an hour and a half, but we've shot for two and a half or three hours. That's a good proportion. The actors warm up and, like a good fullback, get better as they work more. But that's a lot of work, and they can use a breather. Many eat a slow lunch, and since the wall move will take more than an hour, they get a chance to nap. At least I hope they're napping.

When the AD calls lunch, I head for my dressing room. My Achilles tendons ache a little, because I've been on my feet for about four hours. I find it hard to sit down on set. I long ago stopped drinking coffee all morning. A buttered bagel will do nicely at about eleven. In England, the camera apprentice brings a tray of tea for the cameraman and camera crew, for what is called "elevenses." With the tea is a plateful of greasy bangers, fried bread (fried in the grease of the bangers) slathered with rancid butter, onions, soggy bacon. It's delicious! See what a good mood you're in when making movies?

In my dressing room, lettuce, tomatoes, a hard-boiled egg, and some sliced ham or turkey await me. I'll spread mayonnaise on the lettuce, add ham and tomato inside the lettuce leaf, roll it up and bolt it down. I finish my "meal" in five minutes. And then I go to sleep for fifty-five. I'll be asleep within minutes after lying down, a technique I learned in the army during World War II. Again, after all these years, I wake up about a minute before lunch hour is over and go back on set.

With the walls moved, it's time for a new setup. The actors are called. They are usually out of costume, and their makeup needs repair from whatever they did during lunch hour. We start by walking through the new shot. Again I tell them not to work full out. We make sure all props are placed. Then, with stand-ins watching carefully, we go through the shot again, only this time for camera. I've chosen the lens and actually watch the scene, operating the camera myself. I'm not good on the wheels, but I'm not bad either. If the camera moves during the shot, we mark the camera positions with tape on the floor. Sometimes there are eight or ten camera moves in a shot, so that the moves have to be numbered on the floor. Camera height changes are also marked. In addition, places where the actors come to rest are marked with tape, a different color of tape used for each actor. The stand-ins take over so Andrzej can start lighting, and the actors head back to their dressing rooms to get ready.

The afternoon passes quickly. The amount of work done in any day depends on so many factors. However, as long as the actors don't have time to get bored, I consider it a good day.

Around three o'clock, the production office sends down a copy of the next day's call sheet. I check how far along I am with today's planned shooting. If I think I'll get more done, or less, in the remaining time today, I'll have them change the call sheet accordingly. If the actors can get another fifteen minutes' sleep in the morning, I want them to have it.

By four-thirty or so, I'm careful not to start a sequence or shot that I won't be able to finish by five-thirty, which is our quitting time. That repeated shot I made with Brando in *The Fugitive Kind* was an exception only because I thought we'd have it in the can by his usual Take 1 or Take 2. I can always go into overtime, but I don't unless it's absolutely essential. To begin with, I've worked hard all day, and I'm tired. The actors are too. Crews are used to many hours of overtime, so they generally don't start losing efficiency until they've put in twelve hours. I'll try to end shooting for the day around five, but I'll try to get the first setup before I release the actors. If it's a particularly difficult setup, the crew can stay a little later so they can get a good jump on the lighting for tomorrow morning. If walls have to be changed, the grips can stay late to do it.

Then it's on to rushes, then into the station wagon (my teamster had better be at the front door with the motor running) and home. A half-hour nap, a shower, dinner at eight, with a good Brunello, and in bed at nine-thirty. Mentally, I'll review the day. Did I get what I wanted? Do I need any additional coverage? Is there anything I want to reshoot? I don't go out at all during shooting. Sometimes my wife and I will have close friends in for dinner on a Friday night. Saturday, a day off, I still haven't come down from the week's work. It's not too restful a day. But Sunday—with the help of the *Times* crossword puzzle and the acrostic, and, in the fall, football on TV—I relax a little.

If all this sounds like very hard work, let me assure you that it is. And as far as shooting the movie goes, this has been the easy part of shooting. We've been in the studio. We've had total control. There were no distractions. All of that goes out the window when we work on location.

Try to picture the following. In *A Stranger Among Us,* one of the climactic scenes is a shoot-out in the heart of New York's diamond district, on Forty-seventh Street. During the shoot-out, three taxis collide; another car has its windshield shot out and crashes into the tailgate of a truck. The hoods then commandeer a fourth taxi. Melanie Griffith shoots out its windshield, and the taxi mounts the sidewalk and crashes into the window of the jewelry store we'd duplicated in the studio.

Under normal circumstances, considering the difficult and dangerous stunt work, the special effects of windshields being shot out, and the staging of a hundred and three extras, we would allow three or four days to shoot the sequence. The sequence would require sixty-seven setups, and doing twenty setups a day is sensational work. We rarely do twenty in the studio, where everything is under our control.

But we had only one day to shoot the entire sequence. And it had to be a Sunday, because we needed the entire block and to buy out every jewelry store on the block for the day would have been financially impossible. Within each jewelry store, space is often rented to other jewelers, so that would've meant buying out the day's worth of business of two hundred and fifty individual owners. Even if we'd been willing to spend the money, a weekday wouldn't have worked. There is an amazing network of private security on that block. There are untold millions of dollars' worth of merchandise in the stores and vaults. No truck just pulls up and starts to load or unload. If the truck isn't scheduled, it isn't allowed to stop, even if it's delivering bagels to the four or five delicatessens on the block. And most of the trucks are not delivering bagels. Additionally, every store is on an automatic alarm system that opens and shuts the vaults at fixed times. This can't be changed without the approval of the many companies that insure the stores. When we first went scouting locations, there were four of us. We found out later that the private security people had spotted and photographed us the first day we walked down the block. Four guys walking slowly up and down both sides of the street, stopping in front of each store and talking, taking a picture and then moving on—that's not a welcome sight on Forty-seventh Street.

How did we do it? I'm still not sure. At five o'clock on Saturday afternoon, as usual, all the merchants moved their jewelry into the vaults. The vaults locked automatically at 6:30 p.m. Inside each store, a small army of our set dressers replaced the real jewelry with fake junk mounted on cards. They had to finish by 6:30, at which time most of the stores' alarms would switch on automatically. One group of set dressers ran into problems, but the store owner was wonderful. Because he loved movies, and because we gave him $2,500, he called the security company and the insurance company, and they retarded his alarm system by fifteen minutes.

Then our trucks started moving into the street. Movie trucks are conspicuous because they carry logos of the rental companies that supply us with equipment. They had to be disguised as the normal trucks that work the street. I wanted our trucks on the shooting street because we simply wouldn't have time to go running to another block for new film, lights, cable, nets, grip stands, and all the other things you need for shooting.

I used three cameras. That meant I could get three shots on each setup. That reduced the number of setups to twenty-two plus one, still a formidable amount of work. We had daylight by 7:00 a.m. Of course, we'd begun work while it was still dark. A dolly track was laid in the one spot that wouldn't be seen in the first five shots (fifteen setups). The extras reported at seven, already costumed and made up. That was a big job in itself, because a great number of people on that street are Hasidim. These are the ultra-orthodox Jews who wear beards and payess (sidecurls). Their heads are usually covered by fedoras or large-brimmed felt hats. We sewed the sidecurls right into the hats so we wouldn't have to apply them individually.

By 8:00 a.m., the AD had staged the extras. I called for the principals, and we rehearsed the entire sequence once—without stunts, of course, but with the stunt drivers walking their action.

We had one great piece of luck. The day turned out to have a solid cloud cover. As long as it lasted, we'd have a gentle flat light. We could shoot in any direction, and the light would be the same. This was enormously helpful with three cameras. If we'd had a sunny day, we would have had to use "fill light" (for the reasons explained earlier). Also, whether I like it or not, the sun keeps moving. Light at eight o'clock is very different than it is at noon. Buildings throw different shadows and reflections. To "match" the light in different shots taken at different times with three different cameras would've been nearly impossible, and shots that aren't matched can look like hell once they're cut together.

We had one lousy piece of luck too. Normally, the Pulaski Day parade goes up Fifth Avenue from Fifty-seventh Street to Eighty-sixth. For whatever reason, that year it started at Forty-second Street. That meant that happy Poles, native costumes flapping, bands caterwauling "Beer Barrel Polka," would be marching past our corner at Forty-seventh Street and Fifth Avenue. We placed two big trucks at the end of the block to cut off any view of the marching Slavs. But I knew all sound would be useless and we'd have to add it later. I was just grateful that some of my distinguished relatives from Warsaw, warmed by a few nips of slivovitz, didn't decide to come see if we needed any help.

We started shooting at about 8:45. We finished at 2:30 that afternoon. We were even able to take a half-hour lunch at one o'clock. I slept for twenty-five minutes.

On the next page is the call sheet for that day. Notice the amount of detail. Section 2 contains the notification that the publicity department would have a separate crew shooting us shoot the scene. The publicity department makes up something called the Electronic Press Kit on every movie. It provides the footage for all those fascinating promotional pieces you see on the six o'clock news, promising to take you "behind the scenes of a major motion picture." Note also that we have to shoot the sequence rain or shine.

In section 3, the Xs beside the numbers indicate stunt people and the characters for whom they are doubling. The letter X without a number indicates the stunt coordinator, to whom the stunt people report.

In section 4, the "Props and Special Instructions" section is interesting. Notice "multiple windshields," in case we don't get the shot on Take 1 and therefore need a new windshield. Also instructions to remove the mailbox and the No Parking signs,

```
TITLE CLOSE TO EDEN                                    DATE: SUNDAY 10/6/91
DIRECTOR SIDNEY LUMET              CALL SHEET        SHOOT DAY#: 12
ASST DIR HARRIS/PENOTTI/SMITH   (718)555-1234         CREW CALL: 8:00A
                                                   SHOOTING CALL: 8:20A
```

SET DESCRIPTION	SCENES	CHARACTER	PAGES	LOCATION
: EXT-DIAMOND STORE &	89	1,2,6,15,16,01X,	1-7/8	: 47TH ST.
ST-D				
: ''SHOOT OUT CRASH''		06X,X,016X		: (Betw.5th & 6th
:				: Avenues)
: EXT-DIAMOND STORE &	91	1,2,6	7/8	:
ST-D				
: ''INSANELY GREAT COP''				:
:				:
: IF TIME PERMITS:				:
: EXT-DIAMOND STREET-D	22	1,2,3,9		:
: EXT-DIAMOND STREET-D	45	1,2,4,5		:
: EXTRAS RPT TO NE CORNER OF 47TH & 6TH AVE.				:
: HOLDING AREA: 1211 6TH AVE./'LOWER CONCOURSE'				:

[1]

```
: -----------------------------------------------------------------
: xxxxBE ADVISED ELECTRONIC PRESS KIT CREW WILL BE ON SETxxxx
: ****ABSOLUTELY NO VISITORS OR GUESTS WITHOUT JOHN STARKE'S APPROVAL****
:
: -*-*-*-TRUCKS LOAD IN ON SATURDAY EVENING—OCT. 5TH-*-*-*-
: !!!!!!!!!!!!!!!!!!!! NO COVER -*- RAIN OR SHINE !!!!!!!!!!!!!!!!!!!
```

[2]

CAST		CHARACTER	P/U	M/U	SET
: 1	: Melanie Griffith	: Emily	: P/U @ 6:30A	: 6:45A	: 8:20A
: 2	: Eric Thal	: Ariel	: P/U @ 6:15A	: 6:30A	: 8:20A
: 3	: Lee Richardson	: Rebbe	: W/N	:	:
: 4	: Mia Sara	: Leah	: W/N	:	:
: 5	: Tracy Pollan	: Mara	: W/N	:	:
: 6	: John Pankow	: Levine	: P/U @ 7A	: 7:15A	: 8:20A
: 9	: Ro'ee Levi	: Mendell	: W/N	:	:
: 15	: James Gandolfini	: Tony Baldessari	: RPT @ 7:30A	: 7:30A	: 8:20A
: 16	: Chris Collins	: Chris Baldessai	: RPT @ 7:00A	: 7:00A	: 8:20A
: 01	: JANET PAPARAZZO	: ST.DBL.'EMILY'	:	:	:
: 06	: SPIKE SILVER	: ST.DBL.'LEVINE'	:	:	:
: X	: JACK GILL	: ST.DBL.'TONY'	: P/U @ 7:30A	:	:
: 01	: DANNY AIELLO,JR.	: ST.DBL.'CHRIS'	:	:	:
: 1X	: ANDY GILL	: ST.THUG #1	:	:	:
: 2X	: TONY LUCCI	: ST.THUG #2	:	:	:
: 3X	: NICK GIANGULIO	: HOT DOG MAN	:	:	:
: 4X	: BILL ANGNOS	: ND.CAR DRIVER#1	:	:	:
: 5X	: PHIL NIELSON	: ND.CAR DRIVER#2	:	:	:
: 6X	: JOEL KRAMER	: TAXI CAB DRIVER	:	:	:
: 7X	: PAUL BUCOSI	: PEDESTRIAN #1	:	:	:
: 8X	: GERRY HEWITT	: PEDESTRIAN #2	:	:	:
: 9X	: TED	: PEDESTRIAN #3	:	:	:

[3]

STANDINS AND EXTRAS	PROPS AND SPECIAL INSTRUCTIONS
: STANDINS #1,2,6, RPT @ 7:30A	: CARDBOARD BOXES,HAND DOLLIES,
: -------------------------	: EMILY'S GUN,HANDCUFFS,MULTIPLE
: 103 B.G.RPT @ 7A	: WINDSHIELDS,SHOPPING BAGS,THUGS'
: TO INCLUDE: 10-TRUCK DELIVERY MEN/	: GUNS
: 15-HASIDIM MALES/20-SIGHTSEERS/	: VEHICLES: CRASH TAXI,UPS VAN,
: 50-SHOPPERS/4-DELIVERY BOYS/4-COPS	: 2-PANEL TRUCK,2-PARKED CARS,1-
:	: DARK COLORED CAR,1-WHITE CAR,1-
: 5 B.G. RPT @ W/N	: ALTERNATOR TRUCK,2-POLICE CARS,
: TO INCLUDE: 5-REBBE CORE	: THUG CAR,REBBE CAR,SCHOOL BUS
:	: WARDROBE: ELBOW & KNEE PADS FOR
:	: EMILY
:	: LOCATIONS: ACCESS TO ALL DOORS OF
:	: MODELLS,CONTROL TRAFFIC,GUNFIRE
:	: REMOVE MAILBOX & 'NO PARKING'SIGN,
:	: PRACTICAL AMBULANCE
:	:

[4]

CREW CALL: 8:00A

DIRECTOR: P/U @ 7:30A	SOUND: 8:00A	SCENIC: 8:00A
ASST DIR: 7:30A/6:30A	GRIPS: 8:00A	MAKEUP: 6:00A
SCRIPT: 8:00A	PROPS: 8:00A	HAIR: 6:00A
CAMERA: 8:00A	ELECT: 8:00A	WARDROBE: 6:00A
STILLS: 8:00A	CARPS: PER D.RESEIGNE	COFFEE &: RDY @ 6A
P.A.S : PER J.PENOTTI	DRESSER: PER G.BRINK	LUNCH:
STUNTS: O/C	SPEC EFX: O/C	VIDEO: —

[5]

ADVANCE SCHEDULE	TRANSPORTATION
: MONDAY 10/7/91	: PER T.REILLY/J.NUGENT
: INT-KLAUSMAN'S-D SC.32 (POSSIBLE)	: ---------------------
: IF NOT COMPLETE-THEM:	: P/U S.LUMET @ 7:30A
: SC.45,59,45A,45B,45C,22,14(N)	: P/U M.GRIFFITH @ 6:30A
:	: P/U E.THAL @ 6:15A
: TUESDAY 10/8/91	: P/U J.PANKOW @ 7A
: EXT-REBE HOME & ST.-D	: P/U J.GILL @ 7:30A
: SC.17pt,17Apt,37,54pt,51,53pt,73	:
:	: ---------------------

[6]

because they might interfere with the stunts. Also, sadly, a practical—operational—ambulance. Whenever stuntwork is done, an ambulance must stand by.

"Stunts: O/C" in section 5 means no stunts, because stunts

have been accounted for in section 3. Unlike the teamsters, stunt people don't have to have their instructions repeated.

Because of the time pressure, that Sunday's shooting involved a great many people. But all location work requires a huge crew. Even a small, low-budget picture like *Running on Empty* needed the following for one location day: one grip truck, one electric truck, one prop truck, one generator truck, one makeup and hair truck, and two campers. Campers are portable dressing rooms for the actors. Each contains three compartments, so three actors can share it. I get one of the compartments for my lunch-hour snooze. Every camper requires one union teamster to drive it, so you try to keep the campers to a minimum. Then add the three station wagons that brought the actors to the location. If extras are being used and the location's outside the city, as *Running on Empty* was, a bus must transport them. Each bus has room for forty-nine extras. You must use up to one hundred twenty extras who are union members; if your crowd is larger, you can use local people. Then there's the honey wagon, four portable toilets built into one truck. We're now up to twelve trucks, which means not only twelve drivers but parking problems. So add a teamster captain and an assistant teamster captain. Add one or two additional ADs and three or four additional PAs. Add two station wagons to transport *them.* Add six security men, two per shift, three shifts if you're on that location overnight. Add two to four local off-duty cops to control traffic if you're using streets or need police barricades.

In addition, when on location, we also use a rigging crew. On a small picture, the rigging crew consists of two electricians and two grips. They work in advance of us, the shooting crew. Depending on how much lighting the location will need, they arrive one, two, sometimes three days ahead of us. They place all the major lamps in position. Every minute saved by prerigging means hours saved when the enormous shooting crew arrives.

On *Prince of the City,* we had 135 locations. We had a 52-day schedule. That meant we had to *average* a little over two locations per day! In addition to a rigging crew of four electricians and three grips, we had a clean-up crew. After we finished shooting, a crew of two electricians and two grips came in to take the lights down, since the rigging crew was already working on the next location. Furthermore, if a wall had been repainted, we had to restore it to the original color.

I haven't mentioned the caterer. If we want to hold the lunch hour to an hour, it's essential that food be ready when we break. The lunch hour doesn't officially start until the last man in line on the crew has been served. If you take only a half-hour lunch break, the crew gets paid more. The caterer also keeps us supplied with a steady flow of hot coffee and soup in cold weather and iced drinks and watermelon in hot.

You can see how the numbers start adding up. On *Running on Empty,* a small picture, we wound up with about sixty people on location, not counting cast. On *Prince of the City,* about one hundred and twenty. A large action picture will easily double that crew size. And if many extras are involved, increasing makeup, hair, catering, and props, you can get up to hundreds in crew.

On my pictures, all these organizational problems are addressed two to three weeks before shooting. I take the chiefs of all the departments—props, electrical, grip, scenic artist, AD, locations, stunts (if used), teamsters, rigging—on what we call the survey trip. We visit every location. We discuss where the trucks will park, what lamps are to be used, where they will be placed, what has to be redecorated or repainted for the look of the picture. If it's a period movie, television antennas and air conditioners have to be removed and then replaced. For this, of course, we have to get permission from the people who live there. On *Daniel,* a period picture, lampposts had to be replaced. Everyone makes copious notes, to be followed religiously.

The Morning After was the only picture I've shot in Hollywood. We weren't shooting out of a major studio. We used a pickup crew of freelance technicians. On the survey trip, I noticed that the teamster captain wasn't taking notes. I figured he had a good memory. But when I arrived on location on the first day of shooting, the trucks were parked exactly where the camera would be aimed for the first shot. The AD called the teamster captain over and asked what the hell had happened. The captain said that he'd never been on a picture where what was planned was actually carried out. He wasn't around for the second day.

Night shooting is even more difficult. *Everything* will have to be lit artificially. The rigging crew is usually joined by the electricians of the shooting crew at least four hours before nightfall. This is because cables have to be laid from the lights to the generators. Because the generators make a lot of noise, they're usually placed fairly far from the set so they don't interfere with the sound department. It's a lot easier and safer to lay the cables in daylight, when you can still see. Many weeks of night shooting exhausts everyone, including the crew. You really can't sleep during the day, or I can't. But there's a wonderful intensity about night shooting. After eleven o'clock, the neighborhood goes to sleep. And here, in the midst of blackness, a group of people are "painting with light," creating something.

We shot *The Seagull* in Sweden. We built Madame Arkadina's

house in a clearing in the woods by a lake. There was only one night of shooting. Gerry Fisher, the cameraman, told me to take a long dinner break, since he'd need about an hour and a half to finish lighting once night had fallen. Cameramen can't fine-tune their lighting until it's completely dark. An hour after nightfall, I drove out to the set. The road led over a hill. As the car came over the crest, I saw below me a small, concentrated, white-hot diamond. Everything around it was black except for this beautiful burst of light, where the set was being lit. It's a sight I'll always remember: people working so hard, all making the same movie, creating, literally, a picture in the middle of a forest in the middle of the night.

8

RUSHES
The Agony and the Ecstasy

At Technicolor in New York, on the second floor of a ratty building surrounded by porn shops, there is an ugly little screening room. It seats about thirty people. The screen is no more than fourteen feet wide. Very often the light from the projectors is hot in the center of the screen and falls off on the sides, giving you an uneven picture. The sound system is to sound what two tin cans and a string are to telephones. Morty, the projectionist, has been complaining for years, but to no avail. When the air-conditioning clanks on, the hum is so loud that all dialogue is inaudible. If the air-conditioning hasn't been turned on for at least a half hour before we come in, the smell of food gets mixed with the odor of chemicals from the lab upstairs. The food smell wafts up into the room from the restaurant on the ground floor. Even before the restaurant leased the space, the room smelled of food. Chinese. I don't know why. The men's room is far away. It's always locked, so that street bums can't get in to mug you. Morty has the key, which is attached to a long, heavy piece of wood. This is where we come to look at yesterday's work. After all that labor, this is where I come to look at yesterday's work and try to estimate how well we did.

It's called "going to rushes" because the lab, in order for you to see the work as quickly as possible, does one-light printing. Most pictures that are shooting in town send their negative to this one lab, where it goes into its chemical bath. Despite many different shooting conditions, a midrange printing light is selected, and all positive prints are made on this one light. Later, greater care will be taken on the final print; but for now, speed is the first priority.

It's always an exciting but terrifying moment. Ossie Morris, the British cameraman, told me that even after having made hundreds of movies, he crosses his fingers each time the lights go down in the screening room as rushes begin.

We straggle in, feet dragging, because we've just finished another tough day of shooting. We arrive at different times because we've come by different transportation. First AD, script girl, cameraman, operator, focus puller, soundman, art director, costume arrive. The editor and first assistant editor are there ahead of us, having brought the film and sound. Very often the second and third ADs come. Sometimes the gaffer (chief electrician) likes to come, or the dolly grip, if there was a particularly difficult dolly shot the day before. Makeup and hair come if there's been a problem or a change. They usually sit near the door, because they arrive late.

Ossie's crossed fingers are by no means unusual. There are more superstitions in this room than a baseball team's locker room when a fifteen-game winning streak is on the line. If I'm shooting in the winter, I'll wear the same sweater every day. I always sit in the front row, so the screen looks bigger. No food allowed. Editor on my right. Cameraman one row behind me and one seat to my left. Wherever people sit that first day, that's where they have to sit for the rest of the picture. No changing.

For whatever reason, producers and studio executives sit in the last row. I'm convinced it's because they hate movies and want to be as far from the screen as possible. Maybe it's because the phone is usually in the back, though nobody makes a call during rushes.

Some actors never come. They hate seeing themselves. (I told you the self-exposure was painful.) Henry Fonda never went to rushes in his whole career. In fact, he rarely saw the movie until it had been out for over a year. But on *12 Angry Men,* he was also the producer, so he had to come. After we'd seen the first day's rushes, he leaned forward, squeezed my shoulder, whispered, "It's brilliant," and fled, never to return. Pacino always comes. He sits on the side, alone, and an icy calm comes over him. He's very tough on himself. If he feels he blew it, he'll ask you to reshoot, if possible; it invariably comes out better. Sometimes actors use rushes self-destructively. They get sidetracked by how they look. The slightest hint of bags under the eyes will send them into a fit of depression. When I see this happening, I ask them not to come anymore. This usually sets off a minor crisis, but I'm prepared to be very tough about it. Some actors contractually have the right to come to rushes.

Actually, actors are no worse than many of the technicians. Rushes provoke a great deal of vanity. Almost everybody is concentrating on his own work. I've seen production designers near tears because a seam where two walls were rejoined was not perfectly repainted. No one else will ever notice it, but they'll talk to the set scenic artist first thing the next morning, to make sure it doesn't happen again. And they're right. Soundmen suffer because of the transfer. On the set, they record on quarter-inch tape. This has to be transferred to 35 mm tape so it synchronizes with the film. This is done at a "transfer house." If the technician at the transfer house is sloppy, you get a bad transfer that changes the quality of the sound. Sometimes the technician at the transfer house gets creative and filters the highs or lows or reduces or raises the volume of the original recording, and the soundman goes crazy. And again, he's right.

In other words, we're there to see if what we intended has ended up on the screen. That's our first priority. And it requires a strange combination of rooting for the film and being brutally honest about its failings.

Good work comes from passion. When I arrive in that room, I can't suddenly make believe that I'm objective. I'm not. Like a field-goal kicker watching the ball approach the uprights, I pray it through. I want it to work. But I have to be very careful while watching. How do I maintain my passion and yet judge realistically whether we achieved what we were reaching for? It's touch and go. Sometimes, during the take, I've been thoroughly convinced it was perfect. And yet at rushes, that same take leaves the slightly sour taste of disappointment in my mouth. Sometimes, during another take, I may feel that perhaps I've settled for something less than I hoped for. And at rushes, it turns out to be wonderful. Sometimes I've thought on the set that Take 2 was better than Take 4, only to discover at rushes that the opposite is true. It doesn't happen often, but it does happen. I think I basically do the same thing that I do when we're shooting: I participate in the scene I'm watching. If my concentration breaks, something is wrong.

Looking at rushes is very, very difficult. Not many people know how to do it or what to look for. Sometimes a take has been printed because I want one tiny moment from it. But I'm the only one who knows that. Editors *must* be able to look at them constructively. They have to have a connection with both the material and the director, and yet be able to maintain their objectivity. Sometimes they have to suspend judgment. The editor may not always realize that I've done a scene *this* way because I intend to play the preceding or following scene *that* way. And I haven't shot that scene yet. It will make dramatic sense only when the two scenes are cut together.

You also have to watch your own inner state very carefully as you come in to rushes. Perhaps today's shooting hasn't gone very well. You're tired and frustrated. So you take it out on yesterday's work, which you're watching now. Or perhaps you've overcome a major problem today, so in an exultant mood, you're giving yesterday's work too much credit.

The first day of shooting *The Wiz* was one of the most difficult I've ever had. We were down at the World Trade Center. The lighting of the enormous set had taken three nights, and construction had taken three weeks. For the scene of Dorothy arriving at the Emerald City, we had to be able to change the color of the entire set from green to gold to red.

On the day of shooting, the dancers worked to a click track. A click track is an electronic metronome that gives the dancers the exact beat of the orchestra's tempo. In addition, they hear bar counts on it—"One-two-three-four-five-six-seven-eight," "Two-two-three-four-five-six-seven-eight," "Three-two-three-four-five-six-seven-eight," etc.—so the dancers know exactly where they should be choreographically. For the rushes, the editor had replaced the click track with the track of the orchestra's recording.

Because it was the first day of rushes, and because there are so many more departments on a musical movie, the screening room was packed. We weren't at Technicolor's screening room. It was a much larger room, with excellent sound.

As the first shot came up, the orchestra burst out through six speakers. The shot was quite spectacular, an overhead shot of sixty-four dancers at a high point in the choreography. Led by the irrepressible and wonderful Joel Schumacher, who'd written the script, people started cheering and clapping! As shot after shot came up, the enthusiasm grew. It felt like the Broadway opening night of *My Fair Lady*. And yet my heart kept sinking. Whenever a shot came up of anything in the red sequence, it revealed a hot, white center where the lamp had been placed. We could see the source of the light, one of the basic no-no's of lighting.

When rushes were over, people left the screening room, bubbling with delight. Sitting there, I could feel Ossie Morris behind me, not moving in his seat. Tony Walton, the art director, and Dede Allen, the editor, didn't move either. I turned to Ossie. His head was in his hands. "My balance was wrong. I should've used smaller units and opened up more. Then we wouldn't have had the hot spots." His voice was almost choking with tears. "Can we reshoot the red sections?" he asked. I knew we had only four nights at the World Trade Center. It had been incredibly difficult to get permission to shoot there in the first place. The Trade Center is run by the Port Authority of New York and New Jersey, a bureaucratic nightmare. Even with the help of two United States senators, we had barely eked out the four nights. I said, "Ossie, we'll try. We've got to finish the sequence. If there's any time left over, we'll reshoot whatever we can." Ossie and I had done four pictures together. We were close. We hugged, and I drove him home. But we couldn't get the extra day we needed from the Port Authority. We were able to reshoot only one of the shots. So in the final editing, I reduced the red sequence as much as I could.

Unfortunately, we ran out of time on that picture. With time, most technical problems *can* be fixed. But on a picture called *Child's Play*, something much graver happened. *Child's Play* had been quite successful on Broadway. It was a gothic murder mystery, set in a boys' parochial school. As a play, it had a spooky, theatrical effectiveness that worked. But around the third day of rushes, I realized that I'd completely deceived myself. Whatever I'd seen in the script and throughout the preproduction period simply didn't exist. Whatever had worked about it as a play remained in the theater. What once appeared scary now seemed totally unthreatening. A terrific gothic melodrama on stage had become a mundane mystery with a telegraphed resolution. It couldn't transfer to the screen—or at least I couldn't do it. What was worse, I couldn't fix it. I didn't know what the problem was, so I couldn't solve it. All I knew was that it was fake, it wasn't going to work. And I was facing seven more weeks of shooting. And worst of all was the fact that I was the director. So I couldn't tell anybody. If there was any hope of salvaging a movie out of the mess, everyone needed his confidence. I didn't want to shatter it. There was nothing to do but bite my lip for the next seven weeks and try to make the movie look as professional as possible.

Another movie, which I'd rather not name, had three very high-powered stars in it. But on the second day of shooting I began to realize that the leading actress lacked the tenderness her part called for. She simply didn't have it in her as an actress or a person. She was superb with anger; she had humor. But if she was asked to show the simplest affection for the person playing opposite her, a falseness crept into her acting that was readily apparent, particularly since her acting was otherwise so real and true. My on-set impressions were confirmed at the rushes when the first gentle scene was screened. I talked to the editor. Was my impression correct? He hedged a bit but admitted that the scene wasn't as moving as some of her other work had been.

I reshot her side of the scene. I told her that something had gone wrong in the lab. No difference. Since the movie was fundamentally a love story, I knew that we were in trouble. My mind went racing ahead. How could I compensate for her toughness? Lenses? Filters? Music? Eventually I tried everything.

But for the rest of the movie, I could never go to rushes with a light heart. A basic part of that movie was always going to remain unrealized. Though I continued to "root it home," I maintained a depressed objectivity.

There is another kind of experience at rushes. It doesn't happen as often, because first-rate work doesn't happen as often. But sometimes you feel that something wonderful is happening. I wrote earlier that there are times when a picture takes on a third meaning, a life of its own, which neither the director nor the writer knew was there. Generally, this sense of something special going on happens around the end of the second or the beginning of the third week of rushes. You arrive each evening with more and more anticipation. Slowly you give up any expectations of what you're going to see. You simply sit back with a kind of silent confidence, knowing that what you're going to see will be surprising but right. This feeling keeps growing over the first two weeks, and then you just give yourself over to it. It happened on *Dog Day Afternoon* and *Prince of the City,* among a few others.

When this magic happens, the best thing you can do is get out of the way of the picture. Let *it* tell *you* how to do it from now on. I think it's quite clear by now that my movies proceed with great control and preplanning. But on those pictures when this feeling arose at rushes, I'd slowly jettison a lot of the ideas I'd formed before shooting began. I'd trust my momentary impulses on the set and go with them. If I'd planned a dolly shot for such and such scene, I would shoot it differently when the day came. I wouldn't do this arbitrarily. But if instinct told me to do the shot another way, I'd follow it, without doubts or fears. And the rushes would corroborate that the picture was taking on a new life. But that new life had better be there, or you may wind up straddling two stools, losing what you had in mind in the first place and not achieving the wonder you thought you saw at rushes. The rushes can, and sometimes do, deceive you.

I guess I'm talking about *self*-deception. In any creative effort, I think that's absolutely necessary. Creative work is very hard, and some sort of self-deception is necessary simply in order to begin. To start, you have to believe that it's going to turn out well. And so often it doesn't. I've talked to novelists, conductors, painters about this. Unfailingly, they all admitted that self-deception was important to them. Perhaps a better word is "belief." But I tend to be a bit more cynical about it, so I use "self-deception."

The dangers are obvious. All good work is self-revelation. When you've deceived yourself, you wind up feeling very foolish indeed. You dove into the pool, but there was no water there. Perfect Buster Keaton.

Another great danger in self-deception is that it easily leads to pretension. "My God, did we [or I] do that? Wow!" And you start to believe that you are that *good*. That's the most dangerous feeling of all. I think most of us feel like fakes. At some point "they" will get onto us and expose us for what we are: know-nothings, hustlers, and charlatans. It's not a totally destructive feeling. It tends to keep us honest. The other side of that coin, though, the feeling that we own the work, that it exists only because of us, that we are the vessel through which some divine message is being passed, is lunacy. In fact, that's what happens to Howard Beale (Peter Finch) in *Network*.

There are other rules in looking at rushes. The first is never to trust laughter. The fact that people are breaking up, hitting their heads on the seat in front of them because the shot's so hilarious, means nothing. That shot will still have to be placed between two other shots, one before it and one after it. Also, the people attending rushes are insiders. Their reality has nothing to do with the reality of an audience watching a movie for the first time. Their laughter's the equivalent of what nightclub comics call "band jokes"—jokes that break up the musicians working behind them but are often meaningless to the audience sitting in front of them.

The second rule: Don't let the difficulty of actually achieving a shot make you think that the shot is good. In the finished movie, no one in the audience will know that it took three days to light or ten people to move the camera, the walls, or whatever.

The third rule is the reverse: Don't let a technical failure destroy the shot for you. Obviously, any mechanical error endangers the reality of the movie. And those errors must be eliminated in the future. But you have to keep your eye on the *dramatic* impact of the shot. Is there life there? That's what matters.

And the fourth rule? When in doubt, look at it again a day or two later. Have the editor take the sticks off, so you don't know whether it's Take 2 or 3 or 11, because you might be carrying feelings over from when you actually made the shot.

Finally, a basic question remains about looking at rushes: How can you tell when it's really good? I honestly don't know. If you look at rushes cerebrally, staying outside it, you can be wrong. If you "root it home," you can be wrong. So it comes down to what I live with from the moment I've decided to do the picture: I can be wrong. So what? That's the risk. Critics never take it. Nor do audiences, except for the $8.00 they put down. I try to look at it the other way: What if I'm right? Then I might get another job. And that gives me a chance to be right or wrong again. And to go back to work at the best job in the world.

THE CUTTING ROOM
Alone at Last

For many years, *the* cliché about editing was: "Pictures are made in the cutting room." That's nonsense. No movie editor ever put anything up on the screen that hadn't been shot.

However, there are reasons why this cliché arose. In the thirties and forties, directors rarely cut their own movies. The studio system was totally compartmentalized. There was an editing department. It had its chief editor, to whom all the editors reported. The chief editor saw the cut movie even before the director did. In fact, the director might not see his movie until it had been completely finished. He was probably off doing another movie. In those days, directors under contract to a studio did four or five, sometimes six, movies a year. Like everyone else at the studio, they were simply assigned to a new job as soon as they had finished their last one. Sometimes the director would go onto a movie only a week before shooting began. The art department had done the sets and picked the locations, if there were any. The casting department had drawn the cast from the pool of actors under contract to the studio. The camera department had assigned the cameraman, the costume department assigned the designer, etc. The director stepped into a completely preselected operation and picked it up from there. Joan Blondell once told me that when she and Glenda Farrell were under contract to Warner Bros., they often shot two movies simultaneously. They would be on one movie in the morning, then another in the afternoon—all the logistics of scheduling, etc., worked out by the production department.

The editor would cut the movie as it was being shot. When the first cut (the rough cut) was ready, he would show it to the chief editor, who would suggest changes. Then the picture was shown to the producer. After his changes had been incorporated, they would show it to the vice president in charge of production. Finally, all of them trooped into the screening room to show the rough cut to the head of the studio. Then the picture would be previewed (taken to a movie theater out of town, shown to an audience) and, depending on the reaction, recut and put into final postproduction, supervised by the postproduction department. If the director was a studio favorite, he'd usually come to the preview. The writer? Forget it. When I think about it, it's quite amazing that so many good pictures were made.

Out of this system, certain rules, not only of editing but of shooting the picture, were established by the editing department. For example, every scene had to be "covered." This meant it was mandatory for a scene to be shot as follows: a wide "master shot," usually with the camera static, of the entire scene; a medium shot of the same scene; over his shoulder to her (the whole scene); over her shoulder to him (the whole scene); a loose single shot of her; a loose single shot of him; a close-up of her; a close-up of him. In this way, any line of dialogue or any reaction could be eliminated. Ergo, "pictures are made in the cutting room." Obviously, the more successful directors had a little more freedom, but not an awful lot. The chief editor attended all rushes, and if he thought that a scene had not been adequately covered, he often appealed to the vice president in charge of production, or even to the head of the studio, who would then order the additional material to be shot. And the director would shoot it.

In addition to destroying any originality in the shooting of a picture, this system also put actors through hell, because of the endless repetition of the same scene and the seeming importance of taking a puff on the cigarette on the same line in each of the eight camera angles. And each of those angles would, of course, have numerous takes. If an actor "mismatched"—that is, puffed the cigarette on the wrong line—the script girl would write it in her script notes, which were subsequently sent to the cutting room. The editor would often ignore a superior acting take because his job was much easier if he used a take where the cigarette action "matched."

I always tell the script girl to check with me if the actor has mismatched. I have a pretty good idea of how I'm going to edit a scene while I'm shooting it. The mismatch might not matter. If I get into trouble later, I can almost always get around it with a little hard work, going frame by frame between the outgoing shot and the incoming shot until I find the frame that will make the cut work.

The same limitations applied to the audio side. One of the rules that developed was "No overlaps." This meant, for example, that in a scene where two people were yelling at each other, one actor wouldn't speak, or "overlap," while the other actor was still speaking. In fact, on close-ups, the actors had to leave a tiny pause between each other's lines, so that the editor could cut the sound track. Of course, this made it very difficult to get life into a scene that required a fast tempo. This rule was created to make life easier for the editors.

Nowadays we usually cut the track any way we want to. It just takes more work. We have to find the cut not only on the frame but often on the sprocket hole. There are four sprocket holes per frame, so we have to go up and back many times to find the right place to cut. But it can be done. A good place to make an audio cut is on a plosive, a *p* or a *b*. An *s* works well. Most consonants will work as the point where you can splice two different audio tracks together. Vowels are harder because they are rarely at the same vocal pitch and you might hear the difference at the splice or cut. Finally, as much as I resist it, I can always have the actor come in and redo the line in an audio studio. We call this "dubbing" or "looping," for reasons I'll explain later.

When I said earlier that the chief editor could go directly to the head of the studio, I wasn't exaggerating. In the thirties and forties, MGM alone was turning out over two hundred movies a year. That meant that Margaret Booth, the chief editor, saw Irving Thalberg and Louis B. Mayer much more often than any producer or director did. Margaret Booth was a remarkable person. She was bright and tireless, and she loved movies. I don't know if she had any other life. She was made chief editor when Irving Thalberg was running the studio.

Thalberg was considered a genius, though I have no idea whether he was or wasn't. He and Booth would screen the picture endlessly. When they were satisfied with the rough cut, they would preview the picture. Thalberg would then decide what had to be redone. But reshooting was absolutely no problem. All of the sets were stored on the lot, not taken apart until the OK was given. If rewrites were necessary, the writer was under contract and on the lot, as was the director. If for any reason they were unavailable, others could be substituted. The actors were all under contract and therefore available. If they were working on another picture, no problem. Remember Joan Blondell and Glenda Farrell? I was told that over 60 percent of *Captains Courageous,* a good movie with Spencer Tracy and Freddie Bartholomew, was reshot. Even if that wasn't true, it doesn't matter. It *could* have been reshot. All of it. I think Mr. Thalberg had a very good setup. Shoot it, show it, reshoot it if necessary. I wish we could do it today.

I have a warm spot in my heart for Margaret Booth. When I was shooting *The Hill* in England in 1964, she was still chief editor for MGM. By then she was in her late sixties or even older. MGM was being raided constantly by takeover groups and was, if my memory is correct, in its third change of ownership in two years. Margaret was the only person who ever knew what pictures Metro was shooting and what condition they were in. The studio sent her over to England to see the three Metro pictures being shot there. *The Hill* was in rough-cut form, and the other two were still shooting. She ordered whatever cut copy existed of all three pictures to be screened for her, starting at eight the following morning. Mind you, she had just arrived from California. She was an old woman, and eight in the morning was twelve midnight California time. She didn't ask me or Thelma Connell, the editor of *The Hill,* to her screening but said she'd see us at one o'clock that afternoon.

At one sharp, she marched into the cutting room. She said, "You're running 2:02"—the running time of the movie. "I want the picture under two hours." I didn't have final cut in those days. I asked her, nicely, did she feel it was long in any particular place? "No!" she said. "It's a fine picture and a good tight cut. But get two minutes out, or I will." And with that, she marched out.

I was panicked. Once the studio puts its hands on a picture, there's no way of knowing what will finally emerge. It may start with "two minutes" but wind up unrecognizable. Thelma and I sat at the Moviola (a cutting and viewing machine) and ran through the movie again. We found one thirty-five-second cut, and that was all. The next morning at ten-thirty, Margaret was back in the cutting room. I told her what we'd cut, adding that I thought any further cuts would hurt the picture. "What about . . . ?" and she mentioned a shot. I gave her my counterargument. "What about on the shot where . . . ," and she mentioned another shot. Her film memory was phenomenal. She named seven or eight moments, always perfect on where the shot occurred, what took place in the shot, how its beginning or end might be trimmed—and she'd seen the picture only once. At each suggestion, I gave my reasons for keeping the shot as it was. Finally, she said, "Run it for me."

We ran the picture on the Moviola. You have to sit on a high stool because of the height of the screen, which is only eight inches wide. She sat there on the hard, high stool, watching with complete concentration. When it was over, she said, "You're right. Keep it. It's a good picture." We all left the cutting room together, going in opposite directions. Thelma and I headed for the commissary. We were ecstatic, knowing the studio would now leave the picture alone. Arms around each other's waists, we talked animatedly about what a phenomenal film person Margaret Booth was.

That night, around ten-thirty, Thelma called. In a shaky voice, she reported that Miss Booth had called and wanted to see the picture again at eight in the morning. My heart sank. Movies are full of battles you think you've won, only to have to fight them over and over again.

She saw the picture again. Grumpily, she said, "Leave it," and asked me to walk her to her car.

We went into the hall. I asked her why she'd run the movie again. She said, "Yesterday, when you and Thelma were walking down the hall, I thought you were laughing at me." I stopped. I couldn't believe what I'd just heard. I said, "Margaret, I'll argue with you. But there's no way I'd try to con you."

She started to cry. "I know," she said. "You're not one of them. I'm so tired. All those people"—she may have said "bastards"—"fighting over the bones of this studio. None of them know anything or care about pictures. And I'm the only one who knows what's being shot and what will be ready for release at Easter or Christmas. And everybody lies to me while dumping more and more decisions on me. And I have no help. And I've got to go on to India now. We've got a picture there and it's in trouble and I'm the one who may have to pull the plug on them. Last night I felt so tired. And I thought you and Thelma were conning me also."

I opened her car door. I kissed her cheek. She told the driver, "Heathrow Airport." It's the last time I saw her.

Like everything else in movies, editing is a technical job with important artistic ramifications. While it's absurd to believe that pictures are "made" in the cutting room, they sure as hell can be ruined there. So many misconceptions exist about editing, particularly among critics. I've read that a certain picture was "beautifully edited." There's no way they could know how well or poorly it was edited. It might look badly edited, but because of how poorly it was shot, it may in fact be a miracle of editing that the story even makes sense. Conversely, the movie may look well edited, but who knows what was left on the cutting room floor. In my view, only three people know how good or bad the editing was: the editor, the director, and the cameraman. They're the only ones who know everything that was shot in the first place. As good as *The Fugitive* looks (and it looks terrific), I don't know who did what in the editing. One can assume a basic professionalism in the shooting of the movie, and that movie was beautifully shot. But melodramas and chase pictures are not hard to edit if the basic material has been provided. Our old definition of melodrama still stands: making the unbelievable believable. Therefore, as in everything else in the picture, story is the first priority. Edit it for story, but as part of the form of melodrama, edit it as surprisingly, as unexpectedly, as you can. Try to keep the audience off balance, though not to a point where story gets lost. Most editors go about this by editing the picture in a very staccato rhythm, using cuts of four, five, or six feet (a little over two to four seconds). But I have seen great suspense created by maintaining a long, slow tracking shot that ends with the leading lady in close-up and a hand suddenly coming in to cover her mouth. If the director hadn't *made* the long, slow tracking shot, it couldn't have been created in the cutting room.

In a review of a movie that Dede Allen had edited, the critic went on about what a brilliant editor she was and how recognizable her style was. If she ever read that review, Dede would've been distressed beyond measure. She *is* a brilliant editor. But she prides herself in doing whatever the picture and director ask of her. She's proud that the movies she edited for George Roy Hill are totally different from the ones she did for Warren Beatty or that she and I have done together (*Serpico,*

Dog Day Afternoon, and *The Wiz).* She wants the picture, not Dede Allen, to stand out. She is selfless. She's "making the same movie."

When we began to shoot *Serpico,* right after the July Fourth holiday, the opening date for the movie had already been set: December 6. This is an incredibly short time to shoot, edit, *and* do all the postproduction (sound, music, answer print). Six months of postproduction is a tight schedule. Three months is insane. But we had no choice. We would shoot in July and August and finish everything else in September, October, and November. For the first time in my career, the editor was "cutting behind me." As I finished a sequence, Dede would start editing it as soon as she had the last shot. Up until then, I had always asked the editor to wait until I'd finished shooting and was in the cutting room, but that way we never would have made the release date. After rushes, Dede and I would sit and talk for an hour. I would explain my choice of takes, and Dede would make her notes. "This scene is about his first moment of fear, Dede. The emphasis should be on . . ." Then she would go to work. As shooting continued, the footage started to accumulate more rapidly than Dede could cut it. She began to assign sequences to her wonderful assistant, Richie Marks, so in essence, two editors were now working behind me.

When I finally finished shooting, I went directly to the cutting room. Many of the sequences Dede had cut realized my intentions better than I could have. Others, particularly those about the women Serpico was involved with, required extensive revisions in the editing. Possibly this was because those scenes weren't the best written and didn't have the melodramatic drive of the police scenes. Whatever the reason, we reedited the sequences as best we could, and we made the schedule. But at all times, under terrific pressure, Dede's devotion to the *work* was what came first. And *that's* the "Dede Allen style."

The first thing I notice when I walk into the cutting room is how quiet it is. Making movies is always so noisy. In the studio, as you're shooting on one set, they're building another. A door opens and you hear that ear-splitting screech of the buzz saws in the carpentry shops; hammers going constantly; the thuds of sandbags being dropped; the hum of conversation among the extras; the squeak of nails being pulled; the shouts of electricians as they focus their lamps. Out on location, of course, the sounds are the normal street pandemonium.

But now, in the cutting room, blessed silence. There's even a rug on the floor. The apprentice is going through the tedious job of recording edge numbers. She usually has a small portable radio, tuned quietly to a classical or jazz station. In the past, I might've heard the comforting clatter of the Moviola as the editor reviewed a shot or a sequence. But now, with electronic editing, even that sound has disappeared.

As I take my coat off, I start to smile. I'm so happy to be here. And if the picture involved a lot of tough location work, I'm tired and therefore deeply appreciative of the calm of the place. No more questions. Peace. Quiet. A time to reflect, to reconsider, to reexamine, to discover, and to enter a whole new technical world that can fulfill and enhance the original reason for making the movie.

To me, there are two main elements to editing: juxtapositioning images and creating tempo.

Sometimes an image is so meaningful or beautiful that it can capture or illuminate our original question: What is this movie about? In *Murder on the Orient Express,* the shot of the train leaving Istanbul had that quality. It had all the mystery, glamour, nostalgia, action I wanted the entire movie to have.

But in a movie, every shot is preceded or followed by another shot. That's why the juxtaposition of shots is such a great tool. In the agonizing, soul-baring fights in *Long Day's Journey Into Night*, the shots kept getting wider and wider as father and son found themselves telling each other the cruel, ugly truths about each other. At the culmination of the fight, two extreme close-ups ended the scene; the frames were so tight that foreheads and chins were lost. The impact of the close-ups was doubled because of the wide shots that had preceded them. In *Prince of the City*, when Ciello was considering suicide, the presence of the sky mattered so much because the sky had never appeared before in the movie. In *The Verdict*, the most important transition in the movie was illuminated by the close-ups of Paul Newman examining a Polaroid photograph. He had taken the picture of the victim, and he watched it develop. As the photograph took on life, he did too. I could feel the present breaking through for a man who, up until then, had been trapped in the detritus of his past life. It was the intercutting between the developing Polaroid and the close-ups of Newman that made the transition palpable.

Nowhere was the impact of juxtaposed images more apparent than in *The Pawnbroker*. Sol Nazerman, the leading character, is going through a profound crisis as he approaches the anniversary of his family's deaths in a concentration camp. Ordinary images in his everyday life remind him more and more of his concentration camp experiences, no matter how hard he tries to block them out. In telling the story of his predicament, we were dealing with two problems. One was to arrive at an answer to the central question: How does memory work? Furthermore, how does memory work when we are denying it, fighting its rush forward into our consciousness? I found the answer by analyzing my own mental process when something

I didn't want to deal with came bursting through to over-whelm the present. After a lot of thought, I realized that the suppressed feeling kept recurring in longer and longer bursts of time, until it finally emerged fully, dominating, taking over all other conscious thought.

Now the second problem was how to show this in film terms. I knew that when these feelings were first stimulated, they arrived in tiny bursts of time. But how tiny? A second? Less? The reigning wisdom at that time was that the brain could not retain or comprehend an image that lasted less than three frames, one eighth of a second. I had no idea how this figure had been arrived at, but Ralph Rosenbloom, the editor, and I decided to play around with it. I don't know this for certain, but I don't think three frame cuts had ever been used before. I'd tried, in other pictures, cuts as short as sixteen frames (two-thirds of a second) and eight frames (one-third of a second).

In one sequence, as he leaves his store one night, Nazerman passes a chain-link fence, behind which some boys are beating up another kid. Images of a relative caught by dogs against a concentration camp chain-link fence start to crowd in on him. I adopted the three-frame recognition rule and made the first cut into the concentration camp four frames (for safety), one-sixth of a second. Originally, I had intended to make the second cut a different image, lasting longer, perhaps six or eight frames (one-fourth to one-third of a second). But I found that this produced too clear a memory breakthrough too soon. I reasoned that if I used the *same* image during the breakthrough time, I could reduce the cut to two frames (one twelfth of a second). Even if people didn't quite understand the image the first time, they would after it had been repeated two or three times. I now had the technical solution for the subconscious memories forcing themselves into Nazerman's conscious mind. If the oncoming image was more complex, I felt free to repeat it in two-frame cuts as often as necessary until it became clear. As the scene continued, I could lengthen the images to four frames, eight frames, sixteen frames, and so on in a mathematical progression until they took over and the flashback could now be played out in full.

The technique reached its ultimate fruition in the climactic scene, when Nazerman is riding in a subway car. Slowly the subway car becomes the railway car that carried his family to the extermination camp. The entire transition stretched over a period of a minute. Starting with two frame cuts, I gradually replaced one car with the other. In other words, as I cut in two frames of railway car, it replaced two frames of the shot in the subway car. When I used a four-frame cut of the railway car, it replaced four frames of the subway car, and so on until the subway car *became* the railway car. As the intensity kept mounting, Nazerman rushed to another subway car to escape the memory. He wildly pulled open the connecting door, and we cut to the filled railway car, proceeding from there to play out the flashback scene in its entirety. There was no escape for him. What made the sequence even more visually exciting was that I shot both the subway car *and* the railway car in a 360-degree pan. With the camera in the center of each car, we rotated a full circle. So when we cut the two different shots together, we could match the same arc of the circle. The picture was always in motion, both in the past and in the present.

By now, we were so confident of the technique that we marked the subway/railway transition on a piece of paper and let the assistant do the physical labor. And it took a *lot* of physical labor. In those days, splicing two frame cuts together meant that transparent tape would be placed over *each* frame, connecting the outgoing and the incoming film. But when we looked at the sequence for the first time on a large screen, we knew we had it. We never changed it from the first time we cut it together.

Within a year after the picture opened, every commercial on television seemed to be using the technique. They called it "subliminal" cutting. My apologies to everyone.

The second but equally critical element in editing is tempo. Every splice in a film changes the point of view, because every cut uses a different camera angle. Sometimes it may simply bounce in from a wide shot to a medium shot or close-up on the same angle. Still, the point of view has changed. Think of each cut as the beat of a visual metronome. In fact, quite often entire sequences are cut in a rhythm that will accommodate the musical scoring that will be added later. The more cuts, the faster the tempo will seem. That's why melodramas and chase sequences use so many cuts. Just as in music, fast tempo usually means energy and excitement.

However, an interesting thing happens. In music, everything from a sonata to a symphony uses *changes* in tempo as a basic part of its form. Typically, a four-movement sonata will change not only its musical themes in each movement, but also its tempo in each movement and sometimes even *within* each movement. Similarly, if a picture is edited in the same tempo for its entire length, it will *feel* much longer. It doesn't matter if five cuts per minute or five cuts every ten minutes are being used. If the same pace is maintained throughout, it will start to feel slower and slower. In other words, it's the *change* in tempo that we feel, not the tempo itself.

For some reason, I still remember that I made 387 setups in *12 Angry Men.* Over half of those setups were to be used in the last half hour of the movie. The cutting tempo was accelerating steadily during the movie but would break into a gallop in the last thirty-five minutes or so. This increasing tempo helped enormously both in making the story more exciting and in raising the audience's awareness that the picture was compressing further in space and time.

On *Long Day's Journey Into Night,* I found that I could use editing tempos to reinforce character. I always shot Katharine Hepburn in long, sustained takes, so that in the editing, the legato feel of her scenes would help us drift into her narcotized world. We would move *with* her, into her past and into her own journey into night. Jason Robards's character was edited in exactly the opposite way. As the picture went on, I tried to cut his scenes in a staccato rhythm. I wanted him to feel erratic, disjointed, uncoordinated. Richardson's and Stockwell's characters were handled for the *picture's* sense of tempo rather than their characters.

In movies where I'm not using tempo for characterization, I am very careful to continually change the pace of the movie in the editing. The use of sustained shots, with no intercuts, is laid out very carefully at the beginning, before shooting begins. If it's going to wind up a long uncut take in the final movie, chances are that I'll want camera movement. That means I'll want a floor that I can dolly on so that I can move freely. In my original conference with the art director, at least sixteen weeks before my entry into the cutting room, I'm already thinking of the tempos of my final cut. I may not use the sustained take in its entirety. I may chop it up. But if I haven't shot it, I can't create it now in the cutting room.

Having used a sustained take in Scene A and/or B, I'll start looking to change tempo in Scene C. It isn't hard to justify this. When I placed the camera in its position originally, I asked myself the question: What do I want to see at this moment in the script and why? Now, in the cutting room, I ask myself the same question. It's easy to find a reason to cut from him to her. In fact, with good performances, sometimes it's painful not to see both of them together, full face, at a particular moment. So depending on what tempo the scene needs in relation to the picture as a whole, I can cut back and forth as much or as little as I want to.

As well as a sense of tempo change between scenes, I think of the tempo change over the arc of the whole picture. Melodramas usually accelerate in their tempo because the stories demand an increasing sense of excitement and tension. But in many pictures, toward the end, I've wanted to slow things down, to give the audience, as well as the movie, time to breathe. This is by no means unusual. The classic last shot in romantic melodrama, a slow pull back and an upward movement of the camera, is by now a cliché. Think of *Casablanca*. Bogart looks at Rains: "Louie, I think this is the beginning of a beautiful friendship." As they move away, their backs to us, the camera rises and dollies back. Our two cynics, now on their way to join the Free French, get smaller and smaller in the frame. Fade out. I remember a series of 20th Century–Fox movies that used that shot, adding the *same* music to it. There was always the "lonely saxophone" or "lonely trumpet" feel about it as the detective trudged home, having solved the case but lost the girl, while the rest of the city slept. I can sing the musical theme for you even now.

There can be other reasons for slowing a movie down. In *Dog Day Afternoon*, the entire point of the picture was summed up when Pacino made out his will about three-quarters of the way through. Here the theme came rushing out at us: "Freaks" are not the strange creatures we make them out to be. We have much more in common with the most outrageous behavior than we ever admit. It was essential that his dictating of the will be quiet, gentle, moving.

Over the course of the editing, we'd slowly been tightening the picture, making cuts shorter, eliminating anything extraneous. In the first half of the movie, on what we thought was the final cut, we shortened it by about four and a half minutes. That's quite a bit of time at a late stage in editing. We hadn't shortened anything in the second half at all.

We ran the picture. Dede Allen and Marty Bregman were happy and wanted to "lock" the picture: freeze the cut and turn it over to the sound department for the final steps of postproduction. But I wasn't happy. We stood outside the screening room at 1600 Broadway, next to a porno movie house, arguing. I felt that the first half had been accelerated *too* much. Not that we'd cut into character or compromised the strength of the picture. But the first half was heavily melodramatic. A bank robbery is, by its nature, an exciting event. By cutting four and a half minutes, I worried that we'd set a melodramatic tempo for the picture, which might make the second half seem slower by contrast. And if that happened, the dictating of the will, the slowest part of the movie, might seem interminable. These things are always in *relation* to one another, never alone.

We talked for about a half hour, standing there on the street as cabs, hustlers, porno customers, and passersby moved past us. The next day, I went back to the cutting room and restored two and a half minutes of the four and a half we had cut. I'll never know if what I had feared about the will scene would've happened. But I do know that slowing the picture down a bit didn't hurt it.

From everything I've mentioned so far, it's apparent that preplanning extends to the editing phase as well. However, one of the joys of the cutting room is that sometimes the editing can help turn a scene that isn't working into one that does. This often involves shortening it. Other times, a shift in emphasis can make a scene more interesting. Because movies are physically larger than life-size, they tend to make the point of a scene or character clearer sooner. In *Daniel,* Daniel is searching for some sane explanation of the cataclysms that have overtaken his life: his parents' executions in Sing Sing and the mental collapse of his sister. There were two scenes where Daniel visits his sister in a psychiatric hospital. The second scene, where he carries his now catatonic sister around the room, wasn't as moving as I'd hoped. I eventually realized that nothing was wrong with the scene. The problem lay in the way the first scene between them had been edited: the scene had emphasized *him.* As a result, the second scene provided no new revelation about him. It seemed redundant. After the first scene was recut to emphasize the *sister's* pain, both scenes played much better. She was very moving in the first scene, and we still had something new to discover about Daniel in the second.

This brings up an important point. I said earlier that there are no small decisions in moviemaking. Nowhere does this apply more than in editing. One of the miracles of film cutting is how a change in reel 2 affects something in reel 10. (A one-hour-fifty-minute movie will be composed of eleven reels: ten minutes per reel.) One can never lose sight of the relationship of cut to cut, and reel to reel.

Generally, during cutting, I screen three reels at a time, as soon as I finish cutting them. Seeing how they play on a large screen, I'll make my notes. If they're extensive, I'll go back and rework the reels immediately. If the changes are minor or technical, I'll wait for my second go-round. I try to keep my screenings of each three-reel batch equal, so I'm not looking at any three reels more than any other three reels, unless there's trouble in a particular three-reel section. Only the editor and I attend these screenings. At this point, I don't want any outside opinions. It's too early.

Knowing that most movies don't deserve to run more than two hours, I rarely go more than fifteen reels (two and a half hours) in my first cut. The scenes are not cut loosely. I try to make each scene as tight as I can. If it's not up to tempo, I can't tell if the scene is playing as it should be.

In the old days, they used to make a "long" first cut. This, again, was done for peace and harmony. One of the most re-peated clichés in movies is: "It'll be much better when you get ten [or twenty or thirty] minutes out." Knowing that this comment was inevitable, the editors would leave the tighten-ing up of the movie until after the chief of the department, the producer, and the head of production had all seen it. That way, each person could feel he'd made a real contribution by asking to get ten minutes cut. Eight minutes would go as each person saw it on the way up the corporate ladder. That still left six minutes to be cut when the head of the studio saw it. Guess what *he'd* say? That's right. The editor would remove the last six minutes, and the picture would now be down to a preview-able length, and each person felt that he'd saved the movie.

I've never understood why directors bring in a three-hour first cut. Almost always it means that they'll have to cut at least one foot in every three, since most studios demand a run-ning time of less than two hours. The main reason for this is economic, since the studios and the exhibitors want a certain number of screenings per day. And in most cases, I must say I agree with them. Movies are very powerful. You'd better have a lot to say if you want to run over two hours. I didn't feel that *Schindler's List* was one moment too long. But *Fried Green Tomatoes?*

A first cut that runs over three hours can really damage a picture. In the desperation to get rid of time, the actors' pauses go, tracking shots are cut in half, everything that isn't bare-bones plot goes flying out the window. Overlength is one of the things that most often results in the destruction of the movie in the cutting room.

We've done the first cut. Now, before screening the entire picture for the first time, we go through it once again. I make my corrections from notes of the three-reel screenings. I want to include every scene, every line of dialogue, and every shot on the first cut, even though I can already get a sense of what lines or even scenes may eventually go. I want to give every-thing its fair shot. But I want every scene running the shortest possible length I feel it can be at the moment.

One day I look up. We've finished the rough cut. Now comes the first critical, nerve-racking test: screening the entire picture. No matter what enthusiasm or despair we feel, we're going to find out whether either is justified. All the self-deception, good or bad, is going to lead us to another poten-tial self-deception, also good or bad. Will the middle of the picture sag, seem slow? Is the picture as moving as I hoped, or as tough? Does the opening work? The ending? The questions, and therefore the fears, are endless.

Before screening the picture, I want at least twenty-four hours away from it. I don't want to be tired or out of my nor-mal rhythm; and since I normally see movies in the evening, I set the screening for eight or eight-thirty. I don't eat or drink anything before. If the writer is available, I ask him to come. The producer. The composer. My wife. And a small, devoted brain trust: five or six friends who know me and my work and wish us both well. There will be plenty of time for objective opinions, not to mention hostile ones, later. Also, it's important that people in the brain trust know the techniques of filmmaking. General opinions are helpful to a point. But it's better to hear someone say, "You know that whole section about forty minutes in, where he's wandering around trying to make up his mind? It's unnecessary. If you can get the time lapse you need in another way, you can drop it." And of course you *can* get the time lapse another way. You don't even have to do a shot of hands spinning on a clock or dissolve from an empty to a full ashtray. You can find an original way of doing it and drop whatever section is redundant.

I like to sit alone during that first screening. Again, in the front row. Because the sound track is in rough shape, the editor usually sits in the back, "riding the pot" (using a volume control to increase low dialogue sections or lower loud ones). Sometimes, if there are long, silent sections, we put in a temporary music track taken off a commercial recording.

As usual, I'm there early. Members of the brain trust are never late. They have changed over the years. Faith and John Hubley used to come. And Bob Fosse. And Robert Alan Arthur. Phyllis Newman comes. And Herb Gardner. Betty Comden and Adolph Green come. Nora Ephron. Ann Roth. Tony and Gen Walton. And Piedy, my wife. That's about it. I owe them many thanks for good and true help over the years. They've sat through some bad times. I once did a picture for David Merrick, *Child's Play*. Among other problems, we were undecided about how to end it, so I had shot two different endings. I ran both on the first screening. As the lights came up, Merrick derisively called from the back, "Is that it?" I called back, "Ask me in that tone of voice again and I'll smack you, you shit-heel." Like all bullies, he hurried out of the room.

But they've sat through good times too. Sometimes one or two have said the magic words "Don't touch a frame." You have to listen carefully. They don't want to be destructive, but you want the truth from them. Often we go out to supper afterward. Good pasta, good wine. And I ask all sorts of questions, large and small. "How did this feel?" "Is that clear?" "Were you bored?" "Were you moved?" This goes on for a long time. The truth is I can almost always "feel" what they thought of the picture as our eyes meet once the lights come up immediately after the screening.

But fundamentally, that screening was for me. Did *I* like it? Have I spent six months, nine months, a year, pursuing something that means something to me? And have I been good enough at my work to put it up there on the screen?

10

THE SOUND OF MUSIC
The Sound of Sound

If the cliché about pictures being made in the cutting room is false, that other cliché, "It'll play better when we add the music," is true. Almost every picture is improved by a good musical score. To start with, music is a quick way to reach people emotionally. Over the years, movie music has developed so many clichés of its own that the audience immediately absorbs the intention of the moment: the music tells them, sometimes even in advance. Generally, that would be the sign of a bad score, but even bad scores work.

When the score is predictable, when it duplicates in melody and arrangement the action up there on the screen, we call it "mickey-mousing." The reference is obviously to cartoon music, which duplicates everything down to Jerry kicking Tom's teeth in. Pictures with scores like that are probably not injured by them. Chances are, the music is not the only cliché in the movie. It's probably loaded with them.

Often it's not even the composer's fault. After the screen-writer, I think movie composers are violated more often than anyone. Everybody thinks he knows something about music and wants to get his two cents in about the score. If the composer comes up with something too original—that is, something the producers or the studio people haven't heard before—the score can get thrown out. I've seen producers make a music editor cut cues, rearrange them, eliminate sections of arrangements, and otherwise tear a score apart until it's unrecognizable. Today, when practically every instrument in the orchestra is recorded separately, it's possible to almost reorchestrate by going back to the original thirty-two- or sixty-four-track recording.

Working in movies is the fatal compromise composers make. In return for very good pay, they go to work writing for a form that can never belong to them. Music, clearly one of our greatest art forms, must be subjugated to the needs of the picture. That's the nature of moviemaking. Even though it may take over completely at certain points, its function is primarily supportive.

The only movie score I've heard that can stand on its own as a piece of music is Prokofiev's "Battle on the Ice" from *Alexander Nevsky*. I'm told that Eisenstein and Prokofiev talked about it well before shooting began and that some of the composing was started before shooting. Supposedly, Eisenstein even edited some of the sequence to accommodate the score. I have no idea whether these stories are true. Even when I hear the music on a record today, I start remembering the sequence visually. The two, music and picture, are indelibly linked: a great sequence, a great score.

I think that that may be one of the indications of good movie music: the immediate recurrence of the visual elements in the picture that the music supports. But some of the best scores I've heard cannot be remembered at all. I'm thinking of Howard Shore's superb scoring for *The Silence of the Lambs.* When seeing the movie, I never heard it. But I always felt it. It's the kind of score I try to achieve in most of my movies. With all the Oscar nominations my pictures have gotten in various categories, only Richard Rodney Bennett's score for *Murder on the Orient Express* received a music nomination. But it was the only picture I've done where I *wanted* the score to shine. As must be clear by now, I feel that the less an audience is aware of how we're achieving an effect, the better the picture will be.

I've sat with my brain trust at Patsy's restaurant, asking them about their feelings after viewing the first cut. Now I will go back into the cutting room and start to reedit. Some of those dialogue lines I didn't like get cut out. Sometimes a whole scene gets removed. Sometimes four, five scenes, a whole reel, get deleted. (It got clear sooner.) Something was dragging in reels 4, 5, 6, 7. Forty minutes of dragging. That's serious. Maybe if we can rearrange some elements, reconstruct a bit. Let this character's story start a little sooner. That helps revive interest. This performance is so good it doesn't *need* that much time. That performance is so bad it *mustn't* have that much time.

In other words, we are editing in the true sense of the word. We are, hopefully, making it better. As I finish the second time around and the third, I screen again. Some of the brain trust may be there, but I widen the audience a little, maybe ten or twelve people. But I pick them carefully, because looking at a picture in this shape isn't easy. The film is scratched, even torn in places. No opticals (dissolves, fade-outs, special effects) have been made. And the audio track particularly is difficult. Dialogue hasn't been equalized, and in some shots you just can't understand what is being said. Since dialogue on exterior locations hasn't been rerecorded (called "looping"), those scenes are especially hard to hear. Sound effects are missing. And of course, the music remains to be scored and placed.

Once we're happy with the cut, I set up two important meetings, one with the composer, the second with the sound-effects editor. The composer was invited to the first screening. The sound effects editor came to the second, and the entire sound effects department (anywhere from six to twenty people, depending on how complicated the job is) came to the third. They're usually a terrible audience. They are listening for sounds only a dog can hear, and they're dreading the amount of work ahead of them.

If the composer was hired before shooting began, perhaps he's attended rushes. He's always invited. But either before shooting or after we have looked at the first cut, we sit and talk in order to decide the critical question: What function should the score serve? How can it contribute to the basic question of "What is the picture about?"

We then adjourn to the cutting room for what we call a "spotting session." We look at the movie reel by reel. I give the composer my feelings about where I think music is necessary, and he does the same. This provides us with a preliminary sketch. Now we review it carefully. Does he have enough room to state the musical ideas clearly? If a musical transition has to take place, have we allowed enough room for it? Very often in melodramas, composers and directors settle for what we call "stings." These are the short, sharp orchestral bursts that accompany the shot of the villain breaking through the door. They last a few seconds. They're supposed to scare the audience. They are such a cliché by now that I don't think they scare anyone. Sometimes music is put in to tide us over a "dissolve," the fading in of a new scene over an old one to show us a change in location or a passage of time. Again, the music will last about twenty seconds. I hate these kinds of cues. I like to make sure that every music cue has enough time to say and do what it's supposed to say and do. We have decided on what we want the music to contribute to the movie. Within the cue itself, there must be enough time to make the idea of the cue work. Short melodramatic bursts or segues from one scene to another simply fill the air with useless sound and therefore reduce the effectiveness of the music when it's really needed.

After the preliminary sketch, we go back over the movie. Now we get very specific about where the music comes in and where it goes out. We time it to the frame. The entry point is particularly critical. The shift of a few frames, or a few feet, can make the difference between whether the cue works or doesn't work. This process takes two or three days. Sometimes if the composer's a really good pianist, as Cy Coleman is, we may bring a small piano into the cutting room and improvise melodies, entrance cues, and general support for the scene.

As I said earlier, I don't want to "mickey-mouse." I want the score to say something that nothing else in the picture is saying.

For instance, in *The Verdict,* nothing much was ever revealed about Paul Newman's background. At one point there's an indication that he went through a rough divorce and was the fall guy for his father-in-law's shady law firm. But we dealt with nothing in his youth or childhood. I told Johnny Mandel that I wanted the deep, buried sound of a religious childhood: parochial school, children's church choir. He was possibly an acolyte. Since the picture was about this man's resurrection, he had to have been brought up religiously, so he would have somewhere to fall from. The picture could then be about his return to faith. The score's function was to provide the state of grace from which to fall.

The Pawnbroker had as complex a score as I've ever worked on. In the opening scene, Sol Nazerman, a Jewish refugee from Germany, is sitting in a suburban backyard, soaking up the sun. His sister asks for a loan so she and her family can take a vacation in Europe that summer. To Nazerman, everything about Europe is a cesspool. He says, "Europe? It's rather like a stink, as I remember." The next sequence shows him driving into New York City, to his pawnshop in Harlem. Those two scenes set up the conception of the score. Earlier, I said that *The Pawnbroker* was about how and why we establish our own prisons. At the beginning of the movie, Nazerman is encased in his own coldness. He has tried desperately to feel no emotion, and he has succeeded. The story of the movie is how his life in Harlem breaks down the wall of ice with which he has surrounded himself.

The concept of the score was "Harlem triumphant!"—that the life, pain, and energy of his life there forced him to feel again. I decided I wanted two musical themes: one representing Europe, the other Harlem. The European theme was to be classical in its nature, precise but rather soft, a feeling of something old. The Harlem theme, by contrast, would be percussive, with lots of brass, wild in feeling—containing the most modern jazz sound that could be created.

I started looking for a composer. I first approached John Cage. He had a record out at the time called *Third Stream,* classical music handled with jazz instrumentation and rhythms. He wasn't interested in doing a movie score. Then I met with Gil Evans, the great modern jazz composer and arranger, but found it tough to get through. Next, I approached John Lewis of the Modern Jazz Quartet, but I felt he didn't really like the movie when I showed it to him.

Then someone suggested Quincy Jones. I knew some of his jazz work from records he'd made on a big-band tour of Norway. We met. It was love at first sight. His intelligence and enthusiasm were inspiring. I found out that he'd studied with Nadia Boulanger in Paris, which meant that his classical background was firm. He gave me other records of his, many on obscure labels. He'd never done a movie score, but that made him even more interesting to me. Very often, because of the nature of the work, composers develop their own set of musical clichés when they've done too many pictures. I thought his lack of movie experience would be a plus.

I showed him the movie. He loved it. We went to work. Talking about music is like talking about colors: the same color can mean different things to different people. But Quincy and I found that we were literally talking the same language in music. We laid out a musical plot that was almost mathematical in its precision. Just like the subway-to-railway-car transition, we moved in steps from the European theme to the final total dominance of the Harlem theme. At midpoint in the picture, they were equally balanced.

It was a magnificent score, and the recording sessions were the most exciting I've ever been to. Because it was Quincy's first movie score, the band that turned out for him rivaled Esquire's All-Star Jazz Band. Dizzy Gillespie, John Faddis (a mere child at the time) on trumpet, Elvin Jones on drums, Jerome Richardson on lead sax, George Duvivier on bass . . . the names kept pouring into the recording studio. Dizzy had just come back from Brazil, and for one music cue he suggested a rhythm that none of us, including Quincy, had ever heard before. He had to sing it with clucks, gurgles, and glottal stops until the rhythm section could learn it. Quincy looked as happy as any man I'd ever seen.

Usually, when we finish recording a music cue, we stop and play it back against the picture. But the level of inspired playing from this band was so high that I told Quincy not to interrupt it. We'd play it back at the end of the day. Nobody even asked for the obligatory ten-minute break every hour. We played right through. At the end of five three-hour sessions spread over two days, we played it against the picture. It was immediately apparent: Quincy had made a major contribution to the movie.

As so often happens when you find a kindred spirit, we went on to do three more movies together. Quincy's score for *The Deadly Affair* was another musical triumph. Based on a John le Carré novella, the movie tells the story of a sad, solitary counterintelligence operator in the British Foreign Office. His wife is constantly betraying him. During the movie, his protégé, whom he trained in espionage during World War II, turns out to betray him both professionally and personally, entering into an affair with his wife.

The two worlds portrayed in the movie, the world of espionage and the almost masochistic love this man feels for his wife, formed the basic concept for the score. But this time, instead of two themes, Quincy created only one: a painfully beautiful love song, sung by Astrud Gilberto. However, as the picture progressed, it slowly turned into one of the most exciting melodramatic scores I'd ever heard. It proved the power and importance of musical arrangements. The theme stayed the same, but its entire dramatic meaning changed as the arrangements changed. Most composers farm out the arrangements. But Quincy did these himself. Again, it was a major contribution.

I've talked about Richard Rodney Bennett's score for *Murder on the Orient Express*. At our first meeting, Richard asked me what sound I heard in my mind for the picture. I said I was thinking of thirties-style Carmen Cavallaro or Eddie Duchin: a really good version of thé dansant, heavy on piano and strings. He not only provided a piano score but also played it himself during the recording session. Richard's a wonderful pianist. He had that Cavallaro style down to perfection. And when I heard the first rehearsal and realized that the train's theme was in waltz tempo, I knew we were on our way to a perfect score.

At one point, Richard suggested underscoring a scene that I felt should have no music. At the recording session, he played it for me. We recorded it and played it back against picture. He was right.

When I haven't been able to find a musical concept that adds to the movie, I haven't used a score. Studios hate the idea of a picture without music. It scares them. But if the first obligation of *Dog Day Afternoon* was to tell the audience that this event really happened, how could you justify music weaving in and out? *The Hill* was also done in a naturalistic style, so no score was used. In *Network,* I was afraid that music might interfere with the jokes. As the picture went on, the speeches got longer and longer. It was clear at the first screening that any music would be fighting the enormous amount of dialogue. Again, no score.

Serpico shouldn't have had a score, but I put in fourteen minutes' worth to protect the picture and myself. The producer was Dino De Laurentiis. Dino is a terrific producer of the old school, wheeling and dealing and somehow always getting pictures financed no matter how wild the idea. His taste, however, tends to be a little operatic, even for me. We argued back and forth. Dino threatened to take the picture to Italy, where I was sure a score would be laid in like wall-to-wall carpeting. I didn't have final cut in those days, and Dino could've done exactly as he wanted.

Fortunately, I'd read in the paper that Mikis Theodorakis, the wonderful Greek composer, had just been released from prison. He had been jailed for left-wing political activities by the ultra-right-wing Greek government. When I reached him in Paris, he'd been out of jail less than twenty-four hours. I explained the situation, telling him about my disagreement with Dino. I said if there was *any* score, I'd prefer that he do it. Happily, he was flying to New York the next day, to see his manager about a concert tour. I told him we'd have a screening room set up so he could come see the picture as soon as he arrived. He drove right from Kennedy to the screening room. His plane was late, and the screening began at one-twenty in the morning.

When the picture ended, he looked at me and said he loved it but it shouldn't have music. I reiterated my problem. I pointed out that Dino would be thrilled to have a composer of Mikis's prestige doing the score, so that we could get away with a minimum amount of music, perhaps only ten minutes. With opening and closing titles consuming about five minutes of music, that would leave very little in the body of the picture. I also pointed out that he could pick up a healthy piece of change. I knew he had to be broke after such a long time in prison. I thought I was being very clever.

Mikis was cleverer still. He pulled from his pocket an audiocassette. He said, "I wrote this little song many years ago. It's a charming folk tune that could work for the movie. Do you think I could get seventy-five thousand dollars for it?" I said I was sure he could. His *Never on Sunday* score was still being played, by Muzak anyway. He said there was another problem.

He would be touring with his orchestra and wouldn't be able to see the picture again or be back for spotting, arrangements, and recording sessions. I told him that I knew a marvelous young arranger named Bob James who would be happy to join him on the road when necessary. I could do the spotting sessions with Bob, who could then arrange the music and conduct the recording sessions. Everybody wound up happy. Dino had his prestigious composer, I wound up with only fourteen minutes of music (including the five minutes of credit music), Bob James got his first movie job, and Mikis took off for his tour a little more solvent than when he had arrived.

Prince of the City was meant to achieve a sense of tragedy in this story of a man who thought he could control forces that would eventually control him. Again, I chose a composer who hadn't done a movie score before, Paul Chihara. Conceptually, Danny Ciello was to be treated always as one instrument: saxophone. Over the body of the picture, his sound was to become more and more isolated, until finally three notes of the original theme, played on sax, was all that remained of the music.

American musicians were on strike, so I was forced to go to Paris to record the music. I bore up as best I could. But poor Paul wasn't even allowed to step into the recording studio. If word got back to New York, he would've been thrown out of the union immediately. They were watching the recording studios in London and Paris particularly. Paul was terrified. He had had a long struggle. Tony Walton had recommended him, and I'd admired his score for *The Tempest,* written for the San Francisco Ballet. Here he was on his first movie, riding with me to the recording studio but not coming in. During lunch, I'd see him across the street, gazing at us like a starving man in front of a bakery window. Every night I brought him a cassette of the day's work. Fortunately, Georges Delerue was conducting. He knew and loved Paul's classical work. No composer ever had a more devoted interpreter.

What makes my work so endlessly interesting is that every picture requires its own specific approach. *Prince of the City* had close to fifty minutes of music. For a picture of mine, that's a lot of scoring. *Long Day's Journey Into Night* was also a picture that I hope achieved tragic dimensions. The musical approach was exactly the opposite. André Previn wrote a simple, slightly discordant piano score, which was used very sparingly. At the end of the movie, Mary Tyrone, thoroughly drugged out, wanders into the parlor, opens an ancient upright, and painfully, with arthritic fingers, stumbles through a piano piece. At first it sounds like a typical piano étude. Then we recognize it as the bare, sparse piano piece that Previn had written and been playing intermittently through the movie. I don't think there was more than ten minutes of music in a picture that ran over three hours.

Two other scores are worth mentioning. Like everything about *Daniel,* the score was easy to conceive and hard to execute. For the only time in one of my pictures, I used music that already existed. I knew from the beginning that I wanted to use Paul Robeson recordings. He was perfect for the period. He was right politically, since it is at a Robeson concert in Peekskill, New York, that one of the leading characters has a traumatic experience. But which songs, and where to spot them? Through trial and error, the score shaped itself. The first song, "This Little Light of Mine," didn't occur until halfway through the picture. It was reprised at the end, when Daniel, restored to life, attends an enormous antiwar rally in Central Park. Only this time around, it was played and sung in a more modern, Joan Baez arrangement. For his sister's funeral, "There's a Man Going Round, Taking Names" worked wonderfully. Editing had to be changed to accommodate the already finished recordings, since the changes we were allowed to make in them were very limited. We could cut a chorus, but that was about it. Two other Robeson recordings were used, including his magnificent "Jacob's Ladder."

For *Q & A,* which took place largely in Spanish Harlem, with the climax in Puerto Rico, I asked Rubén Blades to do the score. He had made a recording of a song he wrote called "The Hit." It fit perfectly into the spirit and the meaning of the picture. Here was a movie about the racism, conscious and subconscious, that governs so much of our behavior. Rubén recorded the song anew, matching the performance to the intensity of the movie. Then he built a full-fledged score based on the song's melody.

The other vital component in the audio power of a movie is sound effects. I'm not talking about the car crashes and explosions of a Stallone or Schwarzenegger epic. I'm talking about the brilliant use of sound in, for example, *Apocalypse Now,* which has the most imaginative and dramatic use of sound effects of any movie I've seen. A close second is *Schindler's List.* I've never done a movie that required such elaborate sound effects. This is partly because many of my pictures have a great deal of dialogue, which forces you to keep sound effects to a minimum.

Immediately after the spotting session with the composer, I have my second meeting, a session with the sound editor and his entire department. If possible, we try to come up with a concept for the sound effects. I don't know what was discussed on *Apocalypse Now,* but a concept was clearly at work: to create an unearthly experience in sound, emerging from the realism of the sounds of battle. On *Prince of the City,* we simply started with as much sound as possible, then kept reducing it as the picture went on. On location interiors, there is always an exterior ambience that comes into the set. We added exterior sounds to interior locations (pile drivers, buses, auto horns) at the beginning of the movie. Then we slowly kept reducing those sounds until we played the final interiors, with the least exterior sound possible.

Sometimes a sound can carry a subtle dramatic effect. In *Serpico,* as Pacino tiptoed onto the landing near the door of a drug dealer he was about to arrest, a dog in a nearby apartment barked. If the dog heard him there, could the dealer hear him also?

We again go through the picture, reel by reel, foot by foot. Much of the work is sheerly technical. Because so much work, both interior and exterior, is done on location, we use highly directional microphones. Their spread is about seven to fifteen degrees. The reason is that we want to pick up dialogue with as little background sound as possible. When we go into the studio, we stay with the same mikes, because the quality of the sound would change too drastically if we switched to normal studio mikes. That would create a lot of extra work later on, because we'd have to equalize the two different types of microphones. So a great deal of the discussion is about adding footsteps, or the sound of someone sitting down on a couch, or the scrape of a chair as someone gets up, and so forth—sounds that are lost because of the highly directional mikes. All of this added sound has to be done anyway, in preparation for the foreign versions of the movie. Dialogue will be dubbed by the various foreign distributors, but we are obligated to provide all background sound effects and music.

The sound editor splits the reels among the people in the sound department. This group takes reels 1 to 3, that group reels 4 to 6, and so on. Each group usually consists of an editor, an assistant editor, and an apprentice. But the sound editor is responsible for the overall supervision. A normal sound job takes six to eight weeks. Obviously, bigger pictures need more personnel and time.

Even if no overall concept has been articulated, I like effects that enhance the dramatic value of a scene. In *The Pawnbroker,* Sol visits a woman he has consistently rejected. It is the actual anniversary of the day he and his family were loaded into cattle cars to be taken away to the camps. She lives in a modern complex of buildings that overlook a railroad yard in the distance. On location one could see the railroad yards. We put in the sounds of a railway switching yard, the sounds of engines, of cars being shunted and bumping into one another. Sound loses its distinctiveness when it continues for any length of time. Used behind the whole scene and played at a very low level, it is barely distinguishable. But it's there. And I think it adds to the scene.

On *The Hill,* I asked the sound editor to play one scene in complete silence. When he played it back for me, I heard the buzz of a fly. "I thought we'd agreed that this scene was silent," I said. He replied, "Sidney, if you can hear a fly, then the place is *really* quiet." A good lesson.

The sound editor on *Murder on the Orient Express* hired the "world's greatest authority" on train sounds. He brought me the *authentic* sounds of not only the Orient Express but the Flying Scotsman, the Twentieth Century Limited, every train that had ever achieved any reputation. He worked for six *weeks* on train sounds only. His greatest moment occurred when, at the beginning of the picture, the train left the station at Istanbul. We had the steam, the bell, the wheels, and he even included an almost inaudible click when the train's headlight went on. He swore that all the effects were authentic. When we got to the mix (the point at which we put *all* the sound tracks together), he was bursting with anticipation. For the first time, I heard what an incredible job he'd done. But I had also heard Richard Rodney Bennett's magnificent music score for the same scene. I knew one would have to go. They couldn't work together. I turned to Simon. He knew. I said, "Simon, it's a great job. But, finally, we've heard a train leave the station. We've never heard a train leave the station in three-quarter time." He walked out, and we never saw him again. I bring this up to show how delicate the balance is between effects and music. Generally, I like one or the other to do the job. Sometimes one augments the other. Sometimes, as here, not.

Sound effects have also developed their own clichés over the years. Can there be a country night scene without crickets? A dog barking in the distance? How about a pile driver in a tense urban scene? Slowly, progress is taking some of the clichés away. Phones in an office no longer ring, they purr. Computers have replaced typewriters, fax machines for teletypes. Everything grows quieter and colorless. Car alarms are a great help, but they're just as annoying on-screen as they are off.

Everything becomes creative if the person doing the job is. It's true as well for something that seems as mechanical as sound effects.

11

THE MIX
The Only Dull Part of Moviemaking

Life has a cruel way of balancing pleasure with pain. To make up for the joy of seeing Sophia Loren every morning, God punishes the director with the mix.

The mix is where we put all the sound tracks together to make the final sound track of the movie. It's a job that can be left to sound technicians, but that has its dangers. For example, I've seen mixers raise the audio level of a quiet scene or moment and lower the audio level of a loud scene or moment. The result is that the shadings in a performance have been evened out to the point of dullness. As I've repeatedly said, a technician can help or hurt.

The mixing room is usually quite large. It has a big screen, cushioned seats, maybe a pinball machine to while away the hours when sound tracks have to be changed. Some directors like darts, others pitch pennies against the wall. The room is

dominated by a console that looks and feels like something out
at SAC headquarters in Omaha. The console contains sixty-
four channels. Each channel has its own sound track placed
on it. Each channel also has many equalizers. Equalizers are
tiny dials that can vary the tonal output of each channel.
The equalizers can reduce or emphasize the high frequencies,
midrange frequencies, or low frequencies in each track. With
some additional equipment, they can even eliminate frequencies. The tracks are broken down into three sections: dialogue,
sound effects, music. We don't usually put up the music tracks
until everything else on the reel has been mixed. We start with
the dialogue.

Depending on how well the original dialogue was recorded,
we can have anywhere from four to a dozen or more dialogue
tracks. If there are two characters in a scene that was shot on
an interior location, their tracks might be quite different. For
example, the character standing near the window might have
a lot more traffic and general exterior sound on his track than
the character in the center of the room. The exterior sound
has to be reduced on that track and sometimes added to on the
other actor's track. We call this "balancing" the two tracks. On
exteriors, these problems are more severe. His side of the scene
was shot at a different time of day than her side of the scene. So
he'll have buses, jackhammers, and noon whistles on his track.
Her track will have none of those sounds. But it will have pi-
geons, trucks, and subway rumblings. These two tracks have to
be equalized and balanced.

Even in the studio, tracks come out with very different
sound qualities. Her side was shot in a part of the set that had a
ceiling; his had none. The two tracks will be markedly different
and now have to be equalized in tonal quality, not in extrane-

ous noise. This is done with those tiny little dials, which subtly add or subtract frequencies, from the very low to the very high.

When tracks are beyond rescue or a word is unclear, we "loop" it. The actor comes into a recording studio. The scene or line is placed on a repeating film loop. The original sound is fed into an earphone. The actor then says the line in the quiet of the studio, trying to get exact lip synchronization. There is an editor in charge of looping called the ADR editor.

Generally, I try to avoid looping. Many actors can never recapture their performance, because the process is so mechanical. But some actors are brilliant at looping and can actually improve their performances. European actors are particularly good at it. In France and Italy, they usually shoot without synchronous sound and loop the whole performance in a sound studio later. I'm constantly amazed at how superbly actors can adjust to technical demands.

Let's say we have six dialogue tracks. Track A: his. Track B: hers. Track C: his looping. Track D: her looping. Track E: an off-camera maid's voice. Track F: a voice on the telephone. I sit there with the dialogue editor, going up and back on the same sentence, sometimes the same *word,* removing noise, equalizing tone, balancing. It's a four-minute scene. That's 360 feet. We will spend perhaps two hours equalizing it, sometimes more. During the two hours, we will have gone over the same 360 feet anywhere from seven to twenty times and more, getting it clearer, sharper, brighter.

Then we move on to sound effects. The highly directional microphones we use are excellent for dialogue, but now every clothing rustle has to be reinforced, every footstep. Sometimes we put in new footsteps because the original ones have too much background noise and therefore, in balancing, we will be forced to add background sound to the other tracks, making the whole scene noisier. These added natural sounds are called Foleys, and the editor in charge is called the Foley editor.

Scenes of violence, whether car crashes or battles or fires, can use all sixty-four tracks on the board or even more. A simple car crash can easily have twelve sound-effects tracks: glass breaking, metal tearing, metal folding, tires on macadam, tires blowing (two tracks), impact (three tracks, one of them timed a frame late so that it can have "echo" added to it), car doors popping open (two tracks), one overall crash effect to provide body for the basic sound. The last would be played at a very low volume, allowing the specific sounds to dominate.

Each one of these effects will have to be equalized, the volume levels set and recorded. Today many of the effects are prerecorded on digital CDs, which supposedly saves time. But you'd better have a wonderful effects editor, because once placed on the CD, the effects are pretty well locked in. You can easily change where they occur, but it's harder to change the effect itself. I've noticed that with every technical advance, mixes take longer and longer. When I first began, an entire reel had to be mixed in one take. If a mistake was made at 880 feet, we had to go back to the beginning and start all over again. We'd rehearse all day and usually go for a take at the end of the day. But we finished a movie in twelve to fourteen days. Now four weeks of mixing is quite normal.

Every technical advance has brought added problems. Since Dolby came in, the Dolby technician had better line up the Dolby equipment correctly, or the whole reel will have to be redone. Dolby came in because of music recording. In order to have more control, music engineers began using more and more microphones at the recording session. I've been at sessions where each instrument has its own microphone! In a way, this almost eliminates the need for a conductor, because the dynamics of the recording can be adjusted in the mix-down (reducing the existing thirty-two tracks to four or six for the final mix). The engineer can raise the volume of the strings here, a piccolo there, brighten the piano so its sound cuts through more.

The only problem with each microphone recording on its own tape was that we ended up with sixteen, thirty-two, or sixty-four separate tapes! As a result, one could hear a high-pitched sound (called tape hiss). The hiss was caused by the magnetic heads of all the recorders touching the tapes. When Koussevitzky was recording with the Boston Symphony, there were four or five microphones, placed over general sections of the orchestra, with another mike to capture the entire orches-tra. All the microphones were fed onto one tape. No tape hiss there. But now, with anywhere from sixteen to sixty-four mikes, there sure was. The Dolby process simply took all the tapes and suppressed them so that the tape hiss was lost in the upper frequencies. Soon, in movies, because of the equaliza-tion problems between Dolby-recorded music and non-Dolby sound recordings, we had to start using Dolby on dialogue, even though only one or two tracks were being used. Then we had to add Dolby to sound-effects recordings. Talk about the tail wagging the dog!

When stereo was added, all tracks were automatically dou-bled. The stereo process divided 10 percent of the sound be-tween the left and right speaker channels and directed 90 percent to the center speaker. Those proportions were for a simple interior dialogue scene. We could spread the sound to 33 percent in each speaker or dominate with the left speaker, move to the center, then to the right on bigger, more complex sound scenes (the stagecoach moving from left to right; though there's nothing wrong with the sound in the 1939 *Stagecoach,* when all sound came from one speaker placed behind the center of the screen). In *Dog Day Afternoon,* we kept careful directional fidelity, with one crowd gathered on the left side of the block and another crowd on the right side. Each crowd's sound always came from the same speaker.

By now, of course, Dolby was in the driver's seat. "Surround Sound" was added. Now we had three speakers behind the screen, two more on the left side of the theater, and two on the right. A closely guarded secret about all this is that you hear the correct balance only if you're sitting in the center of the theater. On the left or right side, those speakers tend to dominate. On a badly mixed picture, a door slamming shut can sound, for those people seated close to the side of the theater, like a cannon going off. In a badly maintained theater, I've heard 60-cycle hum in speakers when no other sound was coming through them. The basic 110-volt AC power line moves the electrons at 60 cycles. If a transformer is close to the power source (and all speakers have transformers), the 60 cycles produce an audible hum. Crackling, caused by dirt on the sound head, can also be heard. I've been in theaters where the coding that directs the sound to various speakers has been malfunctioning, so a madness of voices is calling to me from every place except where the mouth is. Ah, progress. What used to cost about 5 percent of the below-the-line cost of a movie is now at least 10 percent. And rising all the time. We'll see what happens to costs now that digital mixes are being used.

A lot of this came about because the studios, in their endless pursuit of the youth market, were trying to match the quality of recorded music that the kids were buying—a useless pursuit, in my opinion. They're either going to a movie for *that* experience or listening to a record for *that* experience.

The one pleasure in a mix comes when the music is added. Suddenly, the tedious effort seems worth it. Mind you, sitting in that mixing room, we have run the movie, foot by foot, at least seventy-five times, often more. Everything about the movie has become incredibly boring. My favorite scene now looks like something starring Chester Morris as Boston Blackie. Paul Newman has become Tom Mix (no pun intended), and Jane Fonda might as well be ZaSu Pitts. If the names are unfamiliar, go to your favorite video store and ask for their oldest talkies.

But the music starts to pump life back into the picture. Our original sixty-four tracks have been mixed down to six: strings; woodwind; brass; rhythm (without percussion); percussion; and piano, celeste, harp. But hold it! I can't hear that word "Guilty!" when the jury foreman said it. We worked hard getting the word clear, equalizing it. The oboe, which has many frequencies in the same range as the human voice, is the culprit. We try raising the volume of the word. That sounds forced. It should be the gentle whisper it was. We dip the woodwinds, but then we hear the orchestra falling off. If only we could lower the oboe for that one word. And of course, we can. We go back to the original thirty-two-track recording. At exactly 121 feet, 6 frames into the cue, we dip the oboe by 2 DBs (decibels—a unit of sound volume). We put the new mixdown up. We hear "Guilty!" perfectly. And it only took about four hours, or seventy-two pinball games.

12

THE ANSWER PRINT
Here Comes the Baby

Again, a darkened room. How many hours, how many days, have I spent in dark rooms, looking at this movie? Sitting next to me is the timer. He works for Technicolor. His job is to "grade" the final printing of the movie. I'll explain the process a little later.

Timers are very busy people. This one has flown in on the red-eye, arriving at Kennedy at six-thirty in the morning. We meet in the screening room at eight-thirty. He'll be taking the four o'clock back to Los Angeles.

He has his coffee and a blueberry muffin in front of him. No bagels for these guys. They're all George Gentile. On the console is a notepad. Under the screen sits a footage counter. He will make his notes, reel by reel, using the counter: this shot is too dark, that too light, this too yellow, that too red, too blue, too green, there's too much contrast, too little contrast, it's too muddy (a combination of wrong color and wrong density and/or contrast), and so on. Every scene, every shot, every *foot* of film is analyzed, reviewed. I'm always amazed at the film memory these timers have. Days and weeks later, in a phone call between us, I'll mention that Dustin's close-up in front of the Korean grocery store is still too blue, and he'll remember the shot and exactly where it is in the reel. His eye is extraordinary. He'll see a subtle overall yellow that's taking the photographic bite out of an entire scene. It'll be the first time I've noticed it. But now that he's pointed it out to me, I can't see anything else. *Everything* starts looking yellow.

The process of color printing is complicated. I'll try to explain it as best I can. Basically, the color negative contains the three primary colors: red (called magenta in the lab), blue (called cyan), and yellow. Except for a process called "preflashing," which is rarely used (we mentioned it earlier, speaking of *The Deadly Affair*), most of the time nothing is done to the negative delivered by the cameraman. The lab develops it to a standard set of formulas.

It's in the *printing* of the positive that variations become possible.

Once he's returned to California, the timer sits in front of a computerized color analyzer called the "Hazeltine." He feeds the negative into the machine and sees a positive image of the picture on a TV screen. Since electronic color is quite different from chemical color, his judgment is crucial. By adding or subtracting yellow, blue, or red, he can vary the color balance almost infinitely. He can also lighten or darken the image (we call it "density"). He's been instructed by me and/or the cameraman on what we want to achieve visually. When he feels he's achieved what we talked about on the Hazeltine, he enters it into the computer tape that will control the timing of the printing lights. For example, he might wind up with Yellow:

32; Magenta (red): 41; Cyan (blue): 37. The tape is transferred to the timing machine. On a roll of unexposed positive film stock, the tape instructs a white light to go through three prisms of yellow, magenta, and cyan in exactly the time proportions and to the density that the timer entered on the tape: 32, 41, 37. And that's why he's called the timer. The positive stock then moves directly into the chemical bath, just as it would in still photography, and the positive print emerges— what we call the answer print.

Once the color balance is correct, an interpositive is made from the answer print. Then an internegative is made from the interpositive. All release printing going into theaters is made from the internegative. The original negative goes into a vault. It is extremely valuable. In fact, sometimes the original negative is the actual collateral for the bank loan that financed the picture.

The color printing can undo or augment a great deal of what was done in the original photography. For example, I've described what we wanted to do with color in *Daniel.* Everything in Daniel's past was done with filters, turning his childhood life with his parents into golden shades, warm and protective. Everything in his present life was blue, since in essence he'd buried himself with his parents. As the picture continued and Daniel came slowly back to life, his present existence took on more warmth, more life, and therefore a more natural photographic quality. His past became less amber as he acquired distance and resolved the pain and conflict that the past evoked in him. By the end, the colors of the picture were completely natural. Daniel's past and present were now one. He had returned to life.

It was critical that the final timing of the print follow the concept of the original photography. Much of what is done in the camera can be undone in the lab. If a "blue" scene (Daniel's present) had yellow and red added to it in the printing, it could wind up too "normal." The same could happen to the "golden" or "amber" scenes (representing Daniel's past) if blue was added to them. This wasn't only a question of mood. The flashbacks to his early life appeared throughout the picture. The strong color identification was also letting the audience know where we were in time. The timer had to know clearly what our intention was, otherwise he could have defeated the entire style of the picture.

Everything that the cameraman, the production designer, and I have done to create a visual style is affected by the timing. As has happened all through the making of the picture, once again a technician is central to its success or failure. Phil Downey, at Technicolor in California, was a pleasure to work with. After two minutes of conversation, he could translate the intention into the timing of the movie. I don't think I ever went through more than three attempts with Phil in getting the print correct. On the other hand, John Schlesinger once told me he had to go through thirteen prints on *Midnight Cowboy* before the lab got it right.

There's a great danger in this. The answer print must be made off the original negative. Every time the negative is handled, there is a risk of dirt and damage. Damage is almost impossible to repair. My heart is in my mouth whenever the negative is touched. John must have been going batty.

As Phil finishes each print in California, he sends it to me. I call him with my notes. By the third print, I know that the next one will be *it!*

How can I describe the feeling of watching the answer print for the first time—the beauty of it, the cleanness? It's amazing how dirty the work print has become over the months, but now it's fresh and new. Dissolves are in the movie now, night scenes *look* like night: the reds, the blues, and, when the density is correct, the blacks! One of the signs of a good print is the richness of the blacks. Every movie looks like a masterpiece when the answer print is viewed for the first time.

One last test remains. When we finished the mix, the sound track existed on a strip of magnetic track just like the track in your audiocassette, only much wider. We call it, naturally enough, the magnetic track. Now it must be transferred to film, to what we call the optical track, so that it, too, can be married to the answer print. The magnetic track is run through an electric "eye" that transforms the magnetic impulses of the tape to visual patterns on a piece of film negative. We now combine the optical negative with the visual internegative, so the sound track will be printed out on the answer print. If its density is off, sound can be affected. I take the answer print back to the sound studio. We put the final mixed magnetic track on one channel and the answer print, with its optical track, on another. We run them both together, switching up and back between them to make sure no audio quality has been lost going from magnetic to optical. A tiny bit is always lost, but they should be just about identical.

There's nothing left to do now. The movie is finished. It's time to turn the picture over to the studio.

13

THE STUDIO
Was It All for This?

I'm not "anti-studio." As I said back at the beginning of the book, I'm grateful that someone gives me the millions of dollars it takes to make a movie. But for me, and I think for other directors, there is enormous tension in handing the movie over. Perhaps it's due to the fact that this is the picture's first step on its way to the public. But the real reason, I think, is that after months of rigid control, the picture is now being taken over by people with whom I have very little influence.

I don't know what makes a hit. I don't think anyone does. It's not the stars. My own movie *Family Business* starred Dustin Hoffman, Sean Connery, and Matthew Broderick. It died. So did Hoffman's and Warren Beatty's *Ishtar*. Kevin Costner and Clint Eastwood in *A Perfect World* did no business, but Eastwood alone chalked up major grosses with *In the Line of Fire*. The inconsistencies of box office grosses in relation to stars are endless. And yet the salaries for individual stars keep rising, until many of their fees could finance an entire picture.

Nor is it the genre. Westerns were beyond the pale until *Dances with Wolves* became a hit, and then seven more followed. Baseball pictures were out of the question until *Bull Durham.* Then we got a whole string of them. At the moment, cop pictures are out of fashion, but that, too, will change.

In the thirties and forties, studios controlled the financing, the production, the distribution, and the exhibition of movies. Most studios owned their own theaters. They ran double features, two movies at each showing. The bill was changed once a week, which meant that each theater showed four movies a week. MGM, making two hundred pictures a year, was able to keep its theaters filled with only its own product. There was no way of measuring the financial success of each movie, since the accountants could allocate as much as they wanted of the gross to each feature on the double bill. Unless the *whole* double bill did no business, either picture could be made profitable by the studio's allocation. In 1954, the Supreme Court ordered the studios to divest themselves of their theaters on the grounds that their ownership of the theaters gave them an unacceptable monopoly. By the end of the fifties and through the sixties, many studios were in a precarious situation. At one point, 20th Century–Fox had to cancel a picture I was about to begin because it was out of money. I was to start the movie in March, but its big Christmas release, *Hello, Dolly!,* had done poorly at the box office. That's how tight its cash flow was. The canceled picture was *The Confessions of Nat Turner,* based on Bill Styron's book.

Many of the studios fought television as hard as they could. But slowly they realized the enormous financial potential that was being offered to them. Some of the more financially strapped studios began selling off their old libraries of films to the networks. Then other sources of income became possible with cable television.

Today it's again getting hard for movie companies to lose money, though they still manage. What are called ancillary rights now provide them with great protection for their investments: videocassettes, cable television, free television, airline in-flight use. And of course, international rights outside the United States and Canada represent about 50 percent of the total gross. And each country has *its* video rights, to bring in further income. In addition, many of the studios have bought their way back into theater ownership. As I understand it, they stay below 50 percent so as not to violate the Supreme Court order separating the studios from theater ownership. Add in merchandising—the toys spun out of *Jurassic Park,* to name only one example—theme parks built upon blockbuster pictures, and studio ownership of cable television stations. And the financial pages are full of stories about mergers between studios and the television networks. All of this enormous income is based on the movies the studios turn out. One megahit can produce ancillary income of a billion dollars. That's where major stars *do* have a value. With all this potential, the studios are understandably eager to try to bring each picture to as wide an audience as possible. Nothing wrong with that. Except that most pictures can't do that. They're not good enough or bad enough.

As in so many other aspects of American life, audience research is one of the dominant factors in the distribution of movies. When the picture is turned over to the studio, the first thing they arrange is a preview. Of course, the studio has already seen the picture. Some executives might tell you what they think, others hedge it. But any discussion about changes is relegated to the back burner until after the preview.

Most previews are done with the work print and a temporary music and sound track. To get an answer print, the negative of each take used in the movie must be cut. And though we can make almost any changes we want to after the negative has been cut, there is a psychological block, a sense of finality for studios about cutting the negative. As a result, this important preview is often done with an ungraded print that is dirty and scratched, a music track made up of any number of records and selections from the studio's music library, and sound that is barely adequate. The studios maintain there's no real difference from the audience's point of view between previewing that way and previewing with an answer print. One executive told me that he'd run a preview with a piece of film inserted that said in white letters on a black background, *Scene missing.* He said the audience laughed and went right on enjoying the picture. I told him I hope he kept the scene out, since it obviously wasn't necessary.

So I'm sitting in a first-rate screening room, with comfortable upholstered seats and state-of-the-art sound and projection. I've flown out to be here when the executives screen the movie for the first time. Often a preview has already been scheduled for that same night or the next. Present are the head of the studio, sometimes the head of the whole company, the vice president in charge of production, his assistant (often a woman), her assistant (whom I've never met before), the head of distribution, his assistant, the chief of publicity, the head of marketing, the person who will be making the trailer, the producers, and two or three others whose functions I never do find out. After a few forced jokes, the houselights dim. The screenings almost always start on time.

At the end of the screening there is silence. The head of the studio or the head of the whole company usually says something polite and encouraging. Nobody's looking for a fight in public. The distribution, marketing, and publicity people leave rapidly. They will communicate their feelings to the head of the studio later. The rest of us adjourn to a conference room. Maybe there's a plate of sandwiches, or fruit and Evian water. The head of the studio speaks first. Then the comments travel down the chain of command, until someone I've never seen before is giving an opinion. There is a remarkable unanimity, with everyone taking the point of view first expressed by the head of the studio. I have *never* heard an argument break out on the studio's side of the table.

Mind you, I don't think this process of waiting for the head of the studio to speak is exclusively the habit of movie companies. I've never been to a top-level meeting at General Motors, but I'll bet it works about the same way.

But nothing is definitely decided. Everyone is waiting for the preview that night or the next. I think previews can be helpful for certain pictures. In a comedy or melodrama, for example, the audience is part of the movie. By that I mean that if they're not laughing at the comedy or not frightened by the melodrama, the movie's in trouble. In comedies, changing the timing of a reaction shot can make all the difference in whether the joke works. But in straight dramas, I think I know better. I might be wrong. Perhaps I'm arrogant. But I went to work to fulfill an idea. If I *am* wrong, I need the Irving Thalberg setup to fix it: sets, costumes, actors, everything I'll need to reshoot anywhere from 5 to 50 percent of the movie. And finally, there are some pictures that we were *all* wrong about, from idea to script to execution. I was wrong, the writer was wrong, and the studio was wrong for financing it in the first place. There's just no way of fixing that.

The limo driver has picked me up, with lots of time remaining before the preview. It is scheduled for seven o'clock, in a suburb I've never heard of. I don't know California traffic, but everyone always warns me about it. Since I've never gotten stuck, I always arrive at the theater thirty minutes early.

When I pull up, a line has already formed. The people have been recruited mostly from shopping malls. Someone has asked them if they'd like to see a movie starring Don Johnson and Rebecca De Mornay. A brief plot outline has also been given. Representatives of the research group conducting the preview hover about.

On the line, every demographic group is represented, depending on the anticipated rating. This picture will surely be an "R," so no one under seventeen is there. The officially designated categories are: Males 18–25, Females 18–25, Males 26–35, Females 26–35, Males 36–50, Females 36–50, Males over 50, Females over 50. It's all very politically correct: a few African Americans, some Latinos and Latinas, Asian Americans. I've never seen any Native Americans. On *Running on Empty,* the head of production decided on an entire audience of adolescents, because the star was the magical River Phoenix, a teenage idol. Never mind that the story was about sixties radicals who were on the run because of a campus bombing. There was no way anyone under twenty-five would even know that these kinds of people existed. Naomi Foner's script was very complex, involving not only the boy's relationship to his parents but also his parents' relationship to *their* parents. The head of production had a teen star, so in his wisdom, that meant a teen audience.

The line moves forward into the theater thirty at a time, controlled by employees of the research group. The audience will number between four hundred and fifty and five hundred. People with clipboards and pencils rush about. I'm not sure what they do. They work for the research organization.

I'm very early, so I have time to look over the audience as they enter the theater. No matter the age group, they all look like enemies. They've come in shorts, T-shirts, and sneakers. The hairdos seem designed to block the view of the person sitting behind them. Little old ladies from retirement homes in Sherman Oaks mingle with forty-year-old musclemen whose beer bellies hang over their shorts. I realize I am tense. Earlier, I had asked the limo driver to drive me around the neighborhood so I could get a feel for it. The trim houses and neat lawns seem to have nothing to do with the cretins waiting for admission.

I enter the lobby. The smell of overdone hot dogs and stale french fries as well as popcorn is overwhelming. The food and candy stands are very elaborate. Video games placed around the lobby are being energetically played by twelve-year-olds.

I see the editor. He came in last night and ran the picture with the projectionist this morning. They checked sound levels and made sure the projectors were in good shape. He tells me the projectionist liked the movie. I feel better. At this point, any support is welcome.

Twenty minutes before the movie's scheduled to start, the theater is filled. Two rows in the back have been taped off for studio personnel. In the middle of the theater, two seats have been taped off for me even though I've come alone. I like to sit in the middle of the house. I can get a better sense and feel of the audience.

Meanwhile, out in the lobby, minor studio executives start

arriving. Again, the forced jokes. A ritual is at work. The last to arrive, thirty seconds before the picture starts, is the highest executive who's coming to the preview.

The noise in the theater is enormous. The audience has been sitting there for twenty minutes. They've eaten, drunk, and gone to the bathroom. They're very sophisticated about previews. They go to a lot of them. Some have come as a group and are sitting together. Often they tend to horse around because they know the people who made the movie are there. They enjoy their moment of power. If the picture plays well, they quiet down. Otherwise, look out.

At seven o'clock or one minute after, a personable young man comes down the aisle and stands in front of the screen. He politely thanks the audience for coming. If it's a work print being screened, he'll warn them about dirt and scratches. Often he'll talk about a "work in progress." He also tells them how important their questionnaires are, because the "film-makers" want to know their reactions. This, of course, turns them all into instant critics and delights them, since they now know that their reactions will affect the final picture. He finishes with a cheerful "Enjoy the show!" and bounds up the aisle. The lights dim, and the picture begins.

One of the most important moments in any movie is the ending. The research people are very anxious to catch the audience before it bolts for the door. So, very often during the last thirty seconds of the movie, a flurry of bodies come down the still-darkened aisle, arms filled with questionnaires, fingers clutching half-sized pencils. They distribute themselves along the aisles. The final music cue—designed to give the audience an emotional lift—is never completed. The projectionist has been instructed by the research group to start bringing up the houselights five seconds before the end and to dump the sound track so our host can call out from the side of the theater, "Please keep your seats. We are handing out questionnaires, which we'd be grateful if you filled out." Blah-blah-blah, as Mamet would say.

I'm the first one up the aisle and into the lobby. The execs huddle in the last row. Slowly, the audience begins to emerge. They have handed in their questionnaires. Some still sit in their seats, diligently trying to express their feelings.

After ten minutes or so, only about twenty people are left. This is the "focus group." They have been picked in advance by the researchers. They are, as you can imagine, demographically diversified.

The group leader asks them to move to the first two rows. The execs come down to the fourth row, so they can hear the comments. And they begin.

The group leader thanks them and asks them to state their first names. Then he asks them how many thought the picture "excellent," then "very good," then "good," "fair," "poor." They respond to each category with a show of hands. There follows a discussion of what they liked about the movie and how much they liked it.

Then comes the big question. He says, "What *didn't* you like about the movie?" Sometimes there is an awkward pause. Then one person suggests something, then another speaks, and in no time there's a feeding frenzy, with the body of the movie as dinner. There are disagreements, wrangling. Stronger personalities dominate. People who liked all of it have nothing to say, so they sit quietly by.

Every comment is being absorbed by the studio people. Later, many of their conversations begin with, "You know, this came up in the focus group, and I've always felt it was a problem." That only one person might have said it doesn't matter.

It's treated as if the entire group voiced the same objection. Every opinion, no matter how wild, is given weight, and suggestions about what needs fixing are directly related to what the execs heard at the focus group discussion.

We've adjourned to a neighborhood restaurant for some food and a drink. But there is something incomplete about the evening. The "numbers" haven't come in yet. The "numbers" are the percentages of the audience that rated the picture "excellent" and "very good." Equally if not more important is the percentage that would "definitely" recommend the movie to others. This is considered a strong indication of whether or not a picture will receive strong "word of mouth," the main ingredient of a successful commercial engagement. The "numbers" can determine a great deal: release date, number of theaters, and, most important, advertising budget. Advertising costs a fortune, both in print and, particularly, on television. After half an hour, an executive is called to the phone and comes back with the numbers written on a napkin.

The next day a report comes in. The detail is amazing. All the questionnaires that the audience filled out have been counted and analyzed. Here is a list of what has been learned from the questionnaires. Excellent, Very Good, Good, Fair, Poor; Definitely Recommend, Probably Recommend, Probably Not, Don't Recommend; Performances, character by character, including supporting performances; Most Liked Character, Most Disliked Character. Then, under "Elements": The Setting, The Story, The Music, The Ending, The Action, The Mystery, The Pace, The Suspense. Then adjective selections: Entertaining, Interesting Characters, Different/Original, Well Acted, Too Slow in Spots. Then comes "Volunteered Comments": The Ending (notice the overlap), Confusions, Slow Parts. Then (I know this seems endless): Scenes Most Liked,

Scenes Least Liked. And every one of these categories is broken down into percentages: Males Under 30, 30 and over; Females Under 30, 30 and over; White, Non-White, Black, Hispanic. (They are behind the times on politically correct names.) Also, as a final statistical fillip, percentages on Good & Violent, Boring/Dull, Not My Type of Movie, Too Silly/Stupid, Confusing, Too Violent.

In the face of this assault, the discussions about what should be fixed, changed, shortened, or redone can become surreal. A producer once asked me if we could cut all the "Least Liked" scenes and leave only the "Most Liked." Some of the cards are literally obscene: "He looks like a faggot." "I'd like to fuck her."

I have no idea what the correlation is between the "numbers" and the eventual financial success of any movie. I once asked Joe Farrell, whose organization, the National Research Group, conducts most of these tests, if he didn't have a breakdown of this vital piece of information. Almost all the major studios use him, so by now there must be hundreds of movies on file. But no. He said he has no such breakdown. In fact, at the beginning of the audience report, the following disclaimer is printed (these are the exact words): "It should be kept in mind that data derived from audience reaction surveys are not necessarily predictive of box-office success or of a film's marketability, and cannot assess how large the potential audience might be. While the survey can provide information on how well a movie satisfies an audience interested in seeing it (playability), it should not be used to gauge how large the potential audience might be, i.e., it cannot assess the 'want-to-see' level within the broad moviegoer marketplace (marketability)." So what the hell use is it?

Clearly, movies are not the only product subjected to market-audience research. Polling has infected every area of our national life. But I can't imagine Roger Ailes ending a report to George Bush or Ronald Reagan with, "However, I can't tell you how people are going to vote."

And in politics, where I am sure the utmost care is taken because there's so much at stake, the mistakes are constant. In the '89 primary campaign, almost all the polls for the Democratic primaries were wrong. In England's last election, the Tories weren't supposed to win. In Israel, no polling even indicated the extent of Labor's victory. In fact, Likud was supposed to just barely win the election. When I try to combine these polling techniques with something as ephemeral as public taste, which movies invoke, it all collapses around me.

Perhaps some pictures have been helped by changes made as a result of these "Recruited Audience Surveys." I don't know, because Mr. Farrell won't tell me. Often, after changes have been made, the pictures are previewed again. The "numbers" go up or down or stay the same. But I wonder how many pictures have been hurt. How many movies went through changes dictated by "Audience Surveys" and lost whatever quality or individuality they might have had? We'll never know.

Finally, however, it's an impossible way to work. Why wait until the picture's been shot and all that money spent? Why not start by "polling" the script that has been *read* by a focus group? Why not vote for cast? How about rushes? After they had seen the rushes of five or ten movies, they could tell me which take to use. The first rough cut? Ah—some studios *already* preview those.

I've tried to examine my own attitude. After all, most heads of studios are not idiots. Perhaps there is something I could learn from this new method. In the past few years, I've previewed and consequently altered the following pictures: *Power, The Morning After, Family Business, A Stranger Among Us,* and *Guilty as Sin.* I never used previews before then, except for *Network.* We previewed that to find out about the laughs. They were all there and then some. Except for minor trims, we didn't touch a frame. Other than *Network,* I never previewed any of my pictures that were successes, critical and/or commercial. I don't want to be unfair. I never previewed lots of flops either. But I've never been able to solve the problems of a picture by making changes that were indicated by the previews. And in the quest for a hit, I made those changes after long talks with studio executives who had thoroughly analyzed the questionnaires and focus-group results. I tried it. It didn't work. Maybe it was me. Perhaps nothing could have helped the movie. I don't know.

Almost always, the changes everyone looks for occur around the ending. When a picture isn't playing as well as it should, most everybody looks to a different last scene or two as the solution to the problem. The reason is *Fatal Attraction.* I'm told that in the original movie Glenn Close killed herself. After it tested badly in previews, a new ending was shot in which Anne Archer shot Glenn Close. The testing results jumped, and the picture became a big commercial hit. But most of the time, fixing the ending can't do the job, because *most pictures aren't very good.* Without ancillary rights, most pictures would lose money. Commercial success has no relationship to a good or bad picture. Good pictures become hits. Good pictures become flops. Bad pictures make money, bad pictures lose money. The fact is that *no one really knows.* If anyone did know, he'd be able to write his own ticket. And there have been two who have. Through some incredible talent, Walt Disney knew.

Today Steven Spielberg seems to. I don't say that at all pejoratively. I think Spielberg is a brilliant director. *E.T.* is a superb picture and *Schindler's List* a great one, in my opinion. But though they are the only two people I can think of who consistently turned out hits, it's interesting that even Spielberg can't automatically do whatever he wants (perhaps that's why he's starting his own company) and that Disney fell on tough commercial times when UPA came upon the scene with a new style in cartooning that made him seem out of date. The short-lived successes of *Gerald McBoing Boing* and *Mr. Magoo* made the Disney cartoon style seem passé. Disney's solution was to create a show for television so he could save his studio.

What are we really talking about here? We're talking about a form that produced *The Passion of Joan of Arc, Zero for Conduct, Godfather* I and II, *The White Sheik, Winter Light.* We're talking about *Dodsworth* and *The Best Years of Our Lives.* We're talking about *A Day in the Country, Mr. Hulot's Holiday, Schindler's List, Greed, The General, Amarcord,* and *8½. Singin' in the Rain, Dumbo, The Bicycle Thief, The Grapes of Wrath, Some Like It Hot, Citizen Kane,* and *Intolerance. Open City, Ran, Public Enemy,* and *Casablanca. The Maltese Falcon, Ugetsu, Rashomon, Fanny and Alexander.* Shall I go on? How many more could be added? How can we ever reconcile this art and the gigantic money machine that it takes to make even one *small* movie in America today? I don't know.

The conflicts don't stop there. I once made a picture called *The Hill.* It's a good piece of work. It's the story of a British prison camp during World War II, but the prisoners are English soldiers who've gone AWOL or been caught selling black market goods or have committed any other crimes while in uniform. It takes place in the prison, located in the North African desert. It's a tough, hard movie, never leaving the confines of the camp except for one quick scene in a café and a minor scene in the commandant's bedroom. Physically, it was as tough a picture as I'd ever made. By the end, I was exhausted.

Long after the ordeal of making it was over, I went to the distributor's office to look at the opening-day ads. It consisted of a full-page drawing of Sean Connery, mouth wide open as if screaming in rage. Above his head, in a "thought balloon" right out of the comics, was a drawing of a belly dancer. Don't ask me why. Was he angry at the belly dancer? But there was more. Across the top of the ad, in big white letters, the copy read: "Eat it, Mister!" I couldn't believe my eyes. Even if it had anything to do with the movie—and it didn't—it made no sense. It was blatant insanity.

That night at dinner, I literally burst into tears. My wife asked what was wrong. I said I was just so tired of fighting. I'd fought for the script, for the right cast, then fought the heat of the desert, the exhaustion, the British rules about extras. I felt like Margaret Booth, who had fought with me about the same picture. And now I was fighting about an idiotic ad.

And that's what so much of making movies is about: fighting. I don't remember the last good ad I've seen. It might've been for *The Hunt for Red October* five or so years ago. Certainly movie advertising is boring and banal compared to other businesses; Colgate toothpaste wouldn't tolerate it, much less IBM or Ford. The trailers in the theaters, a major element when they start polling for the "want-to-see" factor, are filled with the same breasts, kisses, and explosions we saw the week before. The posters in front of the theaters, the press and TV junkets when a hundred people are flown in for coffee and Danish with stars and directors, the made-for-cable "behind the scenes" interviews—it amounts to a stupefying dullness that makes my teeth ache. And the money spent on all this is horrifying. By the way, all TV ads, posters, print ads, even the title of the movie are tested, all "audience surveyed" and, of course, broken down demographically. And yet with all this testing, why do most movies open poorly? If everything announcing the movie was tested, at least the opening day's business should be good, before any word of mouth has gotten out. But most pictures do poor business on their first day.

In addition to polls determining the movie's distribution, some executives have surrendered another area of their responsibility. One studio I know will not green-light a picture unless it stars Tom Cruise or his equivalent. This has two immediate effects. First, the stars' salaries skyrocket. And because major stars are getting ten and twelve million a picture, even supporting actors' salaries rise proportionately. Two to three million dollars is not uncommon now for an actor who was getting $750,000 for a picture. The average cost of a movie is up to $25 million and still rising. The second effect is that the agencies that represent the stars are automatically in a more powerful position. The result is that "packages" are created by the stars' agents. The package will include costar (male and/or female) and director, all of them, of course, belonging to the same agency. This isn't anything new. Many years ago, before it owned Universal Pictures, MCA was the most powerful talent agency in the business. Two of its clients were Marlon Brando and Montgomery Clift. When both were desperately wanted for *The Young Lions,* MCA supposedly forced their client Dean Martin into the movie for the third lead. Though he had a name, he was hardly the actor the other two were. But take one, take all.

In all fairness, I should mention that another company makes its decision to green-light a picture strictly on the basis of script and budget. Then they get the best stars they can.

Over all, they're often more successful than the star-based studio.

The decision to go with stars has some validity because their presence significantly adds to the value of the ancillary rights discussed earlier. But on the other hand, the increase to the cost of the picture is enormous when a major star is involved, and not just because of the salary. A fine, well-known actor I've worked with, but whose pictures have never been particularly successful, asked for and received perks that added $320,000 to the budget. And he got them. That's a lot of money that won't wind up on the screen. The picture will have to gross about $1,200,000 more to pay for that $320,000. It breaks down to something like this: The studio keeps $600,000 of that figure, the theater owners get the other $600,000. Prints and ads are now so expensive, they often cost as much as the movie. So the studio's $600,000 is cut in half. That's what paid for this minor star's limos, secretary, cook, trailer, makeup, hair, and clothes person. With major stars the perks can run double and triple that. Sherry Lansing gave the star, the director, and the producer of *The Firm* each a Mercedes-Benz (the $100,000 model) when the picture turned out to be a huge grosser. Her quoted reason was that "they had all worked so hard." I'm sure they had. But supposedly Tom Cruise's salary was $12 million and Sydney Pollack's $5 million or $6 million. I didn't hear what the producer pulled down, but certainly everyone seems to have been adequately paid for his work. If I were a stockholder, I'd be furious over the sixteenth of a penny lost to my dividend. I mention all this because the heads of studios lead very nice lives. Salaries range from $1.5 million to $3 million a year plus stock options, and the perks are first-rate: corporate jet, luxurious suites when hotels are necessary, the

Concorde to Europe if the corporate jet isn't available, limos and all the other glamorous-sounding things we read about in the gossip columns. If, at the beginning, their decision to go ahead with a movie depends on whether major stars want to do it, and if, once the movie's completed, all decisions about revising, distributing, and advertising the picture are deferred to research groups, what are these executives really responsible for? The most basic decisions have been made *for* them.

Moreover, as far as I know, no studio chief has ever died poor. But an awful lot of writers, actors, and directors have— including D. W. Griffith.

Because of ancillary rights and the anticipated explosion of round-the-clock movie rentals on home television sets, movies are now part of the information highway, at once multinational and a great corporate asset for America. Already one of our highest foreign-grossing products, films have a radically positive effect on our balance of payments. They're now part of the world's economic structure.

Hopefully, the need for more and more movies will be helpful to independent production and the tailoring of movies to smaller, but still profitable, audiences. Already, English film production seems to be reviving after a period where it fell to almost nothing. *My Beautiful Laundrette, My Left Foot, In the Name of the Father, Howards End, The Remains of the Day, Henry V* have all earned excellent grosses in relation to their costs, and additionally have been fine movies. Miramax, Fine Line, Savoy, Gramercy are new distribution companies that are trying to establish themselves by financing and acquiring distribution rights to quality movies. They've been so successful that in 1993 the major studios also joined in the chase for the quality buck. *The Remains of the Day* was a Columbia picture; *Schindler's List,* Universal. *Philadelphia* was Tri-Star; *Six Degrees of Separation,* MGM. *In the Name of the Father* was distributed by Universal; *The Age of Innocence* was financed and distributed by Columbia.

I suppose these trends ought to make me feel optimistic. But they really don't. I've seen these fads before. With a little success, smaller companies tend to want to expand. That means they want to play their pictures in more theaters. And that means they have to go to the majors. Miramax has already entered into an arrangement with Buena Vista, which is owned by Disney. As they get bigger, their distribution expenses will also increase. And at that point, will they still be able to take a chance on *Farewell, My Concubine?* I hope so. The track record for independents is not encouraging. A few years ago, DDL (Dino De Laurentiis), Vestron, Lorimar, Corsair, Carolco, and Cannon tried to establish themselves as independent financing and/or distributing companies. They've all disappeared or been absorbed by the major studios.

The need for more movies to feed increased cable TV need is supposedly promising more choice, more production, more room for new talent. But will it ever happen? I don't think so. The erosion of the power of the networks—ABC, CBS, and NBC—caused by the new cable companies has not yet improved the quality of programming anywhere in television. Despite some fine specials on HBO and Turner Broadcasting, the general quality of cable and free TV keeps sinking steadily like a foot in mud. As for the "cultural" channels, how many ocelots licking their young can you watch in a week?

The MGM logo, famous for its roaring lion, also bears the motto *Ars Gratia Artis* ("Art for Art's Sake"). The irony of this is now doubled. First, art had to make money. And now it has to satisfy the National Research Group.

Movies have become a vitally important part of enormous

financial empires. And it seems that this trend will continue to grow. So what is it about movies that compels *The New York Times* to publish the list of the week's ten highest movie grosses every Tuesday? And, now, the New York *Daily News* and the New York *Post* to compete by publishing the same information one day earlier? Why is it that the Cannes festival in May, which is nothing more than a glorified sales convention, elicits worldwide coverage of a quarter-million-dollar party thrown for Schwarzenegger or Stallone? Why is it that I can literally spend a year going to one festival a month, starting in Delhi in January and ending in Havana in December? It's not just the grosses. The mergers taking place along the "information highway," or Sony and Matsushita buying into software, represent far larger financial empires than a movie grossing one hundred million dollars. I think it's because movies are the only art form that uses *people* to record something that is literally larger than life. Records don't do this, nor do books or any art form I can think of. Notice the operative words: art form.

Finally, movies are an art. I believe that no combination of the highest-grossing movies would attract the attention that movies have without the work of Marcel Carné, King Vidor, Federico Fellini, Luis Buñuel, Fred Zinnemann, Billy Wilder, Carl Dreyer, Jean-Luc Godard, Robert Altman, David Lean, George Cukor, William Wellman, Preston Sturges, Yasujiro Ozu, Carol Reed, John Huston, Satyajit Ray, Orson Welles, Jean Renoir, Roberto Rossellini, John Ford, William Wyler, Vittorio De Sica, Martin Scorsese, Ingmar Bergman, Akira Kurosawa, Francis Ford Coppola, Elia Kazan, Michelangelo Antonioni, Jean Vigo, Frank Capra, Bernardo Bertolucci, Ernst Lubitsch, Buster Keaton, Steven Spielberg, and so many others. These are the people who have made movies an art form, who have driven movies on a two-track course. At the same time that *Batman Returns* grosses forty million dollars on its opening weekend, *My Life as a Dog* is moving four hundred and twenty people to laughter and tears in a small theater. The amount of attention paid to movies is directly related to pictures of quality. It's the movies that are works of art that create this interest, even if they're not on the ten-highest-grosses list too often.

My job is to care about and be responsible for every frame of every movie I make. I know that all over the world there are young people borrowing from relatives and saving their allowances to buy their first cameras and put together their first student movies, some of them dreaming of becoming famous and making a fortune. But a few are dreaming of finding out what matters to *them*, of saying to themselves and to anyone who will listen, "I care." A few of them want to make good movies.

Films Directed by Sidney Lumet

12 Angry Men (1957)
Stage Struck (1958)
That Kind of Woman (1959)
The Fugitive Kind (1960)
A View from the Bridge (1961)
Long Day's Journey Into Night (1962)
Fail-Safe (1964)
The Pawnbroker (1965)
The Hill (1965)
The Group (1966)
The Deadly Affair (1967)
Bye Bye Braverman (1968)
The Seagull (1968)
The Appointment (1968)
King: A Film Record . . . Montgomery to Memphis (1968)
(with Joseph L. Mankiewicz)

The Last of the Mobile Hotshots (1970)
The Anderson Tapes (1971)
Child's Play (1972)
The Offense (1973)
Serpico (1974)
Lovin' Molly (1974)
Murder on the Orient Express (1974)
Dog Day Afternoon (1975)
Network (1976)
Equus (1977)
The Wiz (1978)
Just Tell Me What You Want (1980)
Prince of the City (1981)
Deathtrap (1982)
The Verdict (1982)
Daniel (1983)
Garbo Talks (1984)
Power (1985)
The Morning After (1986)
Running on Empty (1988)
Family Business (1989)
Q & A (1990)
A Stranger Among Us (1992)
Guilty as Sin (1993)

Sidney Lumet's films have received more than fifty Academy Award nominations. He has been nominated by the Directors Guild of America for Best Director seven times. In addition, he has received an honorary lifetime membership in the Directors Guild of America as well as its most prestigious award, the D. W. Griffith Award. In 1993, he received the Lifetime Achievement Award from the National Arts Club. His films have been shown in retrospectives at the Museum of Modern Art in New York, the American Museum of the Moving Image, the British Academy in London, and the Cinémathèque in Paris. He has also been honored by the French government as a Commander of Arts and Letters.

A NOTE ON THE TYPE

Spectrum is the last of three Monotype typefaces designed by the distinguished Dutch typographer Jan van Krimpen (1892–1958), a recipient of the Gold Medal of the Society of Industrial Artists in 1956. Originally commissioned from him in 1941 by the publishing house Het Spectrum of Utrecht, Spectrum surpasses van Krimpen's other faces in both the elegance and versatility of the letter forms but shares with Lutetia and Romulus many qualities characteristic of van Krimpen's designs—fine proportions, sharp cut, and generous counters.

Composed by ComCom, an R.R. Donnelley & Sons Company, Allentown, Pennsylvania
Printed and bound by R.R. Donnelley & Sons, Harrisonburg, Pennsylvania
Designed by Brooke Zimmer